# THE TEQUILA BOOK

MARION GORMAN
&
FELIPE P. de ALBA

cbi Contemporary Books, Inc.
Chicago

Published by Contemporary Books, Inc.
180 North Michigan Avenue, Chicago, Illinois 60601
Manufactured in the United States of America
Library of Congress Catalog Card Number: 77-88532
International Standard Book Number: 0-8092-8175-9

Published simultaneously in Canada by
Beaverbooks
953 Dillingham Road
Pickering, Ontario L1W 1Z7
Canada

To Miguel O. — a friendship issuing from a vibrant sun.

# Contents

# Mil Gracias

We wish to acknowledge warmly the contributions of the following friends to *The Tequila Book:*

Miguel Olea Ortiz, Carmen Lopez Figueroa, Juan D. Orendain, Jaime Ruiz Llaguno, Lionel H. Braun.

Also: *Acapulco News;* Aeromexico — Carlos Baz; Bacardi y Cia — Ernesto Robles Leon, Jose Louis Fernandez Marquez; Gene Barnes; Barton Brands Ltd. — Lester Abelson, Robert Schoenbeck; Earl Blackwell; Brown-Forman Distillers Corp. — William R. Carroll; Camara Regional de Industria Tequilera — Rafael Michel Ochoa.

Dr. Alfonso Manuel Castaneda; Consejo Nacional de Turismo — Miguel Aleman, Miguel Guajardo, Elsa Cano; Foreign Vintages, Inc. — Robert J. Doucette; Eustaquio and Maria Escandon; Raul Garcia.

Glenmore Distilleries Co. — Frank B. Thompson, Jr.; Gavin-Jobson Associates — Robert Amato; Heublein, Inc. — Christopher W. Carriuolo, Bill Elliott, J. Richard Grieb, Harry F. Lavo, Theodore R. Parker, Eric Pierce, Evelyn L. Rumstay, G. William Seawright, Peter M. Seremet, Roger W. Slone, Stuart D. Watson.

Robert Bruce Johnson; Francisco Lopez Figueroa; Alfred Lippman; Enrique Rosete MacGregor; Copeland Marks; Minutiae Mexicana, S.A.; E. Martinoni Co. — C. H. Meuel, Polla Chase; Norman Moloshok; Mr. Boston — Marshall Berkowitz; Annette Nancarrow; Rhoda Nathans; National Distillers Products Co. — Robert Lindquist, Emil Pavone,

Stuart Sax; *Novidades de Acapulco;* Pedro Domecq Mexico — Pedro Domecq, Edmundo Fausto Zorilla, Francisco X. Cervantes; Ramon Charles Perles.

Productores de Tequila de Jalisco; Roberto Ruiz Rosales; Salena Royal; Schenley Imports Co. — Harold Barg, Perry Cooper; Schenley Affiliated Brands — Joel Cohen, Scott Romer, Lenny Schultz; Heine Schondube; Jos. E. Seagram Sons, Ltd. — Seymour Feit, Jack Yogman; Seagram's de Mexico — Hugo Enriquez, Pedro Poncelis, Jose Torres; Seagram Distillers Corp. — Alvin Fleischman, Gerry Friedman; General Wine and Spirits (Seagram's) — Stan Shepherd; Somerset Importers — John E. Heilmann; Teddy Stauffer; Lonsdale F. Stowell.

Tequila Cuervo — Juan F. Beckmann Vidal, Francisco Beckmann Vidal, J. Guadalupe Gonzalez Rubio, Sergio Lopez Herrera, Alea Elena Solano; Tequila Eucario Gonzalez — Alfonso Gonzalez; Tequila Herradura — Gabriela de la Pena de Romo; Tequila Orendain — Eduardo Orendain; Tequila Rosales — Carlos Rosales, Guillermo Rosales; Tequila San Matias de Jalisco — Guillermo Castaneda Pena, Guillermo Castaneda Robledo; Tequila Sauza — Francisco Javier Sauza, Mrs. P. M. Smilgus, Mackenzie Wasson; Tequila Virreyes — Roberto Orendain Gonzalez, Sr.; Tequila Viuda de Romero — Joaquin Gonzalez Chavez, Beatriz Gonzalez de Cue.

The American Distilling Co. — Bernard Goldberg, Joseph C. Haefelin, Carmel J. Tintle; *The Colony Reporter,* Guadalajara; *The News,* Mexico City — Gayle Dorantes, Pepe Romero; The Jos. Garneau Co. — Byron G. Tosi; and Young's Market Co. — Vernon Underwood, Sr., Vernon Underwood, Jr.

Marion Gorman and Felipe P. de Alba

# Part 1:

# The Story of Tequila

At one time the very mention of the word "tequila," that fiery substance from south of the border, conjured up images of hot, dusty cantinos, uncontrollable passions, and swaggering danger. Fear and loathing might best describe the once prevailing attitude: fear of what this magic potion might do to the human body in its grip, and loathing of a vile, hardly civilized drinking habit.

But, just as nonbelievers finally stopped laughing when Columbus promised that the world was not flat, Scotch and bourbon drinkers and wine-sippers practically all over the world — if not completely changing their drinking habits — are at least enthusiastically welcoming the variety and excitement of Mexico's most rousing export. Tequila has become fashionable, and from an increasingly steady sales base it has emerged as one of the liquor industry's hottest sellers.

Our purpose here is threefold: to delve into tequila as a social and business phenomenon; to explore the unique entity of tequila — its history and how it is made; and to offer a whole new way of mixing drinks and cooking — not with the spirits familiar to a gourmet's cabinet and cupboard, but with tequila, maybe the liveliest thing ever to happen to a recipe.

After several years of moderate sales in the United States, attributed largely to Margarita drinkers, tequila really took off in California in 1970, and by 1971 was considered the "in" drink nationwide. It swelled to even greater popularity on U.S. college campuses the following year, showed a 70 percent increase in sales in 1973, and by 1974 was topping all previous tequila records. During that year 4½ million gallons crossed the border, making the United States the largest importer of the world's seventy-two tequila-importing countries. "The Liquor Handbook" tracked the tequila movement to 5,200,000 gallons in 1975, enough evidence that tequila is consolidating its rite and ritual in the U.S. market.

All of this stir is more than a flurry. The liquor industry is staking its money and some long-term commitments that tequila is not a fad, that its gain of devotees is permanent and infinite. Why is it newsworthy that people like tequila? Do we bait the question? Hardly. Before really tasting the drink, who had not heard the taints and taunts of tequila: it is dangerous, unsanitary, hallucination- and convulsion-causing, and, concerning flavor, reminiscent of lighter fluid?

So much for old saws. An estimated 60 percent of tequila drinkers are between eighteen and thirty-four, and for them, tequila and its ambience are today's answer to the 1930s' dry martini. To the other 40 percent, tequila's charisma is perhaps the potion of youth. Youthful people are after everything from the philosophical to the fun, and tequila's real image focuses on their search. When Mick Jagger and the Rolling Stones came to America in 1972, no detail escaped their fans, including their favorite drink, Tequila Sunrises (*see* Chapter 2), and the tequila business hasn't been the same since.

The entity of tequila is also tied to the awakened interest in Indian cultures — their magic, rituals, and art. A major sellout in campus bookstores the past few years has been writer Carlos Castaneda's four-volume work exploring the extraordinary powers of hallucinogenic plants grown in Mexico; while neither tequila nor its plant source is hallucinogenic, there is a related aura of mystery and enigma. And many tequila aficionados when asked say their drink symbolizes a sense of naturalness, of disassociation with the Establishment.

While maligning tequila appears to be a thing of the past, propagating misinformation about exactly what it is, is not. Many avid drinkers of tequila would still define it as fermented cactus juice, or call it, interchangeably, pulque or mezcal, two other native Mexican drinks. The confusion is understandable: pulque and mezcal and tequila are the products of the same plant—the agave. But here the confusion can end, because there are more than 400 known species of the agave, and pulque, mezcal, and tequila are each derived from a different species.

In Mexico the agave plant, so named by Swedish botanist Carolus Linnaeus, is often called the maguey, the generic name ascribed by Spanish explorers. Early settlers in the U.S. Southwest termed some species of agave the century plant, basing this on their mistaken assessment that the plant bloomed once every 100 years. But, in truth, most agaves bloom between eight and twenty-five years, depending on the species. Pulque-producing agaves take ten to twelve years to flower. The species producing mezcal and tequila take between eight and twelve years. Mezcal can be distilled from a number of agave species, but only one produces true tequila.

There is some controversy, but most botanists include the agave, characterized by spiny-margined leaves and flowers in tall, spreading panicles, in the Amaryllidaceae family. The single tequila agave plant, the species *Tequilana Weber, blue variety,* has long, narrow, swordlike leaves and a bluish color—thus its frequent name, the blue agave. For the ancient Indian civilizations, and the Spanish explorers, the plant's leaves were a source of food, cloth, needles, thread, and paper. As ancient implements of torture, the sharp spikes were inserted into living human flesh as penance to the gods.

Several agaves provide the juice, called *aguamiel* (honey

water), fermented for pulque, a viscous milky-looking, mildly alcoholic drink. Pulque is probably the oldest alcoholic beverage in North America—it was the only one made by the early Indian civilizations. These ancient peoples considered pulque to be sacred, restricted its consumption, and gave drunkenness the death penalty. Pulque has remained a regional Mexican drink since ancient times because its natural fermenting agents do not hold up under bottling, thus limiting it to local shipments, almost totally in the cold, central highlands of Mexico—the area surrounding Mexico City.

When the Spanish conquerors arrived in Mexico, during the early 1500s, they thirsted not only for power but also for the familiar distilled hard liquor of their homeland. A reasonable substitute would have to suffice, they must have mused, so these hearty-bodied explorers came up with what we know as mezcal and tequila. The distillation process, introduced into Iberia in the 700s, was already a tradition with the Spaniards, so it was for them simply a matter of finding a suitable plant native to their new surroundings that would provide the necessary raw materials for liquor. Taking note of the Indians making their fermented drink, pulque, from the mezcal (as the agave was known to the Indians), or, as the explorers named it, the maguey, the Spaniards tried distilling the juice of different species until the palatable mezcal evolved—different from pulque because of the species source and also because it is not distilled (only fermented).

Mezcal is produced in several regions of Mexico, primarily circling the big heart of Mexico from Guadalajara up to Torreon, then stretching from Manzanillo to Acapulco to Oaxaca on the Pacific Coast, then skipping over to the far southeastern tip of the country. Mezcal's parent agaves thrive in warmer areas than those of pulque. Like pulque, mezcal is considered a regional drink, but for a different reason. Lacking tequila's distinctive flavor and the quality controls imposed by the Mexican government, mezcal does not compete with other spirits in the world market.

As an interesting side note, it may be mentioned here that it is in some brands of the bottled mezcal that the infamous worm makes its home, and *not* in tequila, as some would swear. The worm is clean and dead and harmless, and it lies in the bottom of the mezcal bottle for no decipherable reason other than tradition and as a sales gimmick. Because someone long ago discovered this particular species of worm in the agave plant, where it spends its entire life cycle, he evidently decided to bury the creature in something akin to its natural surroundings — mezcal.

As mentioned before, if it's not the blue agave (*Tequilana Weber, blue variety*), it might make pulque or mezcal, but it won't make tequila. This is one of the four qualifications issued by the Mexican government for defining, protecting, and controlling tequila production and export. If the beverage meets these qualifications, it is given a *DGN* number. DGN stands for Direccion General de Normas, or bureau of standards of the Mexican government.

The second qualification is geographical. By official government proclamation, the blue agave for tequila can be harvested only in a small, kidney-shaped region — now identified in an official testament dated December 9, 1974 — in the Mexican state of Jalisco and parts of the states of Michoacan and Nayarit. The area includes Guadalajara, and, about forty miles northwest, the town of Tequila, the center of the tequila industry. Almost all of the nearly fifty distilleries are in the state of Jalisco, with a sprinkling operating out of Nayarit.

The third qualification is that the fermented agave juice must pass through two distillations. The fourth and last stipulation requires that the final bottled tequila must contain a minimum of 51 percent distilled spirit of the blue agave; only 49 percent, or less, of the remaining liquid mixture may be the distillate of cane sugar. Distillers vary their formulas anywhere from the legal 51 percent minimum up to a full 100 percent.

Probably the most concise illustration of tequila's

uniqueness is provided by writer Gregory Curtis in his study of
Mexican liquors for *Texas Monthly*. He points out that all
tequila is mezcal, but all mezcal is not tequila. Only one
species of agave, harvested only in one area of the world,
provides tequila, whereas mezcal is derived from any one of
several agaves, harvested in several areas. (The tequila plant
will grow in other soils but will not produce a liquor of
tequila's distinct flavor.) Curtis draws an analogy between
tequila and mezcal and cognac and brandy for further
specificity: all cognac is brandy, from a government-
sanctioned area in France, but all brandy is not cognac.

The landscape of the tequila enshrinement is one of con-
trasts and ruggedness. Don Juan Orendain, who prefers
"Juanito," is a member of a well-established family of
*tequileros* (producers and distributors of the liquor). He
graciously offers a tour for the purpose of *The Tequila Book,*
guiding the writer from the countryside, shaded blue with
agaves, on into the core of the distilleries. Juanito's knowledge
of the entity of tequila is intimate and comprehensive, gained
from his heritage and experience.

The road from Guadalajara to Tequila, the town, narrows
to two lanes most of the way and is trafficked mainly by diesel
and pickup trucks. Along the roadside the modern
developments and chicken farms give way to blue-hazed
flatlands nestled at the base of a seemingly lordly, extinct
volcano called "Tequila Hill" by the locals, last active 2,000
years ago.

The land itself is arid, but there is no irrigation because
agaves thrive on dryness and rot if subjected to much
moisture. Juanito disagrees that the long-ago volcanic lava
made the soil conducive to the agave's growth. Instead, he
cites the land's high acid and silica contents, along with the
dryness, as the decisive factors.

For tequila it can be said that it is here, in the soil, that the
maturation process takes place. The only yield in the life of
the blue agave requires eight to ten years to ripen. It is this
agave heart, the *piña* (meaning pineapple, so named because

of its appearance once shorn of its long, spike-shaped leaves), that will be used to make tequila. Stretching toward maturity, the agave starts out the size of a large onion and grows steadily until it reaches twenty to twenty-five inches in diameter, usually about the ninth or tenth year. At this point the heart weighs between 80 and 150 pounds, and its inner color and texture resemble that of a turnip.

Rarely is there a bad harvest. The tequila agave can survive with very little water and thrives on a heavy rainy season. There could be a bad year due to bugs—two types plague the agaves. One is the "mariposa," a worm that eats into the agave heart; the other is the "piojo arenoso," which is like a louse, millions adhering to the leaves near the heart. To capture the former, the tequileros hire schoolboys to spear the mariposa when they come out to take the early morning sun. To combat the latter, the tips of the pencas (leaves) are trimmed during the 5th or 6th year.

The onion-sized agave seeds appear as sprouts around the base of a mature plant. Field hands trim their leaves, allow the bald sprout to dry for about thirty days, then plant the seed. Planting takes place twice a year, before each of two rainy seasons, one extending from April through June and the second occurring in September and October.

The agaves are neatly rowed three feet apart, frequently with corn, peanuts, or soybeans between them. The corn presents a continuing dilemma, Juanito explains. While, like the peanuts and soybeans, it provides extra income and enriches the soil, it nonetheless shades the agaves from the sun they desperately need.

At almost any given time, more than 100 million tequila agaves, of varying ages, are under cultivation in this sanctioned territory. Individual Mexican citizens may own up to 200 hectares, or almost 500 acres, of agave land. One hectare can accommodate between 2,500 and 3,000 plants, so Mexicans can have between 500,000 and 600,000 plants on their private properties.

Harvesting the mature agave, the act of felling the big plant and chopping the big leaves from the piña, is called *jima,* the harvesters themselves *jimadores.* The jimadores use a long pole, a *coa,* uniquely designed for its special task. Attached to a heavy, hoelike handle, the coa has a short, narrow but strong iron blade on the end for chopping away the heavy, tough, fibrous leaves surrounding the juice-filled agave heart.

When it comes to the agave harvest, some of the modern efficiencies of the twentieth century simply don't matter, or don't work. Because much of the terrain in the tequila region is sloped, mules and burros are, of necessity, still used to carry the piñas to another point for loading onto trucks. Or, from fields near distilleries, the mules make the full trip themselves. These mules, rented as a group called an *atajo,* can each carry about 250 pounds of the precious piñas.

The town of Tequila itself is worth describing. Its name means hill of lava, from *tel* (hill) and *quilla* (lava). The town and its 17,000 inhabitants contrast sharply with the prominence of the area's most important product. A village atmosphere pervades, with an open plaza surrounded by the monolith of the church, a ten-room hotel, and assorted bars, restaurants, and shops. Only the extinct volcano, Hill of Tequila, interrupts the surrounding skyline. As if in single recognition of modernity, TV antennas have dotted Tequila's rooftops for the past five years.

Some tequilero families have added improvements to the town. Cuervo built a kindergarten, and the Sauzas have a grammar school, library, and the one and only paved street to their credit. What wealth Tequila enjoys lies behind deceptively lackluster high-walled facades. Some separate the narrow dirt streets from the elegant colonial haciendas of families named Orendain, Cuervo-Beckmann, and Sauza—all original tequileros. Others open onto the vast courtyards and quarters of the distilleries themselves.

In most of the distilleries, in Tequila and elsewhere in the region, the initial scene is repeated: the courtyards are filled with the piñas deposited by trucks and burros, while workers split these hearts of the agave into halves and quarters to be loaded into the great caverns of steam ovens. In tequila making, some of the distilleries stick to tradition, others have adapted to progress for the sake of efficiency. The older, stone ovens require seventy-two hours for the entire process of loading, cooking, cooling, and unloading the piñas. The newer autoclaves cut this time down to twenty-four hours, or one full day.

The piñas must be cooked to soften their starchy pulp and facilitate the conversion into juice. The cooked hearts which now look like soft, cooked pumpkin go into a shredder, to open up their fibers, then through a series of mills that extract the juice.

Photos in this series courtesy Distileria Tequilena, Bacardi y Cia., Tequila, Jal., Mexico.

The tequila agave plant matures 8 to 10 years before it is harvested for tequila. By law, the plant species must be the *Tequilana Weber,* Blue Variety, and it must be grown within a delimited area contained in the states of Jalisco, Michoacan, and Nayarit.

The harvesting of the mature agave is called the *jima*. The *jimadore* uses a *coa* to chop the big leaves from the heart which is called the *piña,* meaning "pineapple." The pina goes to the distillery for tequila, and the leaves are left on the ground to dry, to be gathered later by the workers for fuel for their homes.

The piñas, weighing from 80 to 150 pounds, arrive at the distillery either by truck or by mule. Most of the distilleries are still located in the environs of the town of Tequila.

In the courtyard of the distillery, the workers chop the big piñas into smaller pieces and load them into steam ovens to be cooked. The ovens are either of stone or steel autoclaves. The entire cooking process (loading, cooking, unloading) takes 72 hours in the stone ovens and 24 hours in the autoclaves.

When the agave hearts (piñas) are cooked, they pass through a shredder and a series of mills that press out the juice. This juice is called *aguamiel* meaning "syrup," or literally, "honey water." The fiber is usually burned.

The aguamiel is piped to fermentation vats, which are made of stainless steel, cement, copper, or wood. There it is combined with cane sugar and yeast and allowed to ferment, a process requiring 48 to 72 hours. The law requires that tequila (if it is to be called tequila) contain 51% juice from the *Tequilana Weber*, Blue Variety agave, and no more than 49% cane sugar.

The law also requires that the tequila ferment be distilled in pot stills. If it were distilled in the tower process, it would not have the same character of tequila and the tax would be much higher. Tequila passes through two distillations. It is drawn from the first distillation at 40 proof and heads and tails (undesirable elements) are removed. Tequila comes out of the second distillation usually at 100 to 110 proof, the maximum allowed by law. (*Below*) Immediately after it is taken from the second distillation, the tequila may be piped into a tank truck for shipment to the United States or other ports, or it may be held in large storage vats. All tequila for export must be analyzed and certified by the Mexican government and the shipment sealed by a government official.

The 100 to 110 proof distillate of tequila is mixed with distilled water to reduce it to the desired proof, usually 90 or 92 proof in Mexico and 80 in the United States. Tequila may be bottled and drunk immediately (its maturation takes place in the plant in the ground). Or it may repose up to six months or so depending on the producer. Aged tequila is called *añejo* and is stored in used wine or spirit casks for 1 to 7 years. (*Below*) For the Mexican market most tequila is bottled at the distillery. For export it is usually shipped by tanks at the 100 to 110 proof level and cut with water and bottled by the importer at destination.

Next the juice is ready for fermenting and distilling, the magical transformation into tequila. It goes into fermentation vats, of stainless steel, cement, copper, or wood, along with the allowable (up to 49 percent) proportion of other sugar — usually cane. A smidgen of yeast completes the mixture, which becomes ethyl alcohol in forty-eight to seventy-two hours. This bubbling fermentation is then pumped through pipes into pot stills. The distillate from the first still is taken at 40 proof, immediately passed into the second still, and is usually taken out at 110 proof — the highest permitted by the Mexican government. The lowest proof allowed is 72. Distillers can determine the proof by controlling the boiling point during the second distillation, or, to lower proofs, by adding distilled water. Tequila sold in Mexico averages 96 proof, and in the United States, 80 proof.

The distillate passes through charcoal filters before storage and bottling. Not all tequilas are bottled immediately. Some tequileros continue vat storage for up to six months, and a small amount is set aside for prolonged aging — for up to seven years. This spirit earns the classification *añejo,* or aged, which, by government regulation, means the tequila must be at least one year old.

In addition to añejo, tequila's remaining three categories include:

1) white or silver, as it comes from the second distillation, with distilled water added to lower the proof;

2) gold, the amber color a result of being stored in oak barrels previously used for bourbon, brandy, or wine — with flavorless caramel sometimes added to correct color inconsistencies:

3) and crema de tequila, a liqueur mixed with almond and hardly available outside of Mexico.

By Mexican government regulation, samples of all tequila leaving the country are government-laboratory analyzed prior to the sealing and shipment of tanks. Tequila for domestic consumption is sampled and tested by the government every month.

The tequila-making process described has slowly evolved from that of the previous two centuries. Tequileros vary in the degrees to which they have changed the mystique of making this elusive potion — from the days of man, burro, and earthen ovens, to the scientific predictability and accuracy of modern equipment, of which Francisco Xavier Sauza has been the foremost pioneer. Seagram's de Mexico hired a staff of engineers to adapt some of their old stone ovens for more modern use; and the hacienda of the tequila Herradura displays numerous artifacts from the early days of tequila's history.

Good-quality tequila, in Juanito Orendain's words, is the combined perfection of six things: high-grade agave and complementary sugar; controlled cooking; good yeast; careful fermentation; knowledgeable adjustments of sediment and negative-flavor factors (called "heads and tails"); and high-quality water.

So, as promised, a whole new way of drinking and cooking — with tequila, the combined perfection.

## TEQUILA MINI-LEXICON

**agave** (ah-ga-veh) — the botanical name for a family of cacti varieties which includes the mother plants of mezcal, pulque, and tequila; there are more than 400 known species. The agave plants for tequila, mezcal, and pulque are different in appearance and in product. The product differences are described below. The plants differ in appearance as follows: The tequila agave has narrow leaves, like swords, which are blue in color. The mezcal leaves are also sword-shaped but wider, like a scimitar, and are greener in color. The pulque agave has the largest leaves of all; the spines are heavy and bend from their weight, and their color is grayish, like ash. "Agave" is a Greek word meaning "admirable".

**aguamiel** (ah-gua-mee-el) — the agave juice, or "honey water," to be fermented for mezcal, pulque, or tequila.

**aguardiente** (ah-guar-dee-en-teh) — the Spanish name for raw alcohol applied to any kind of distilled spirit, including tequila, in its unrefined state.

**añejo** (an-yay-ho) — aged at least one year; thus, aged tequila.

**century plant** — a misnomer applied to a non-tequila species of agave by early Southwest pioneers who thought the plant only bloomed once every 100 years.

**coa** (ko-ah) — the long pole used for harvesting the matured agave heart.

**DGN**—Direccion General de Normas, the bureau of standards of the Mexican Government, responsible for certifying tequila standards.

**jima** (hee-mah) — the act of harvesting the agave.

**jimador** (hee-mah-dor) — the agave harvester.

**limon** (lee-mon) — the lemonlike, limelike citrus fruit indigenous to Mexico and traditionally served with tequila drinks if available.

**maguey** (mah-gay) — the name given the agave plant by Spanish explorers, and still frequently used in Mexico.

**mezcal** (mess-kal) — *Primarily* the generic name for all agave plant varieties, derived from the Aztec language and still the term most generally used today. Also, an alcoholic drink derived from species of agave other than the tequila plant. (The term *mezcal,* applied to the plant or drink, has no relationship, botanical or otherwise, to the terms *mescal, mescaline,* or *mescalito.* Mescal is the name frequently used to denote the peyote or peyotl plant; mescaline is the hallucinatory substance derived from the peyote; and mescalito is a peyote button, or discoid top from the peyote, that is eaten to attain a hallucinatory state.)

**piña** (peen-yah) — the pineapplelike heart of the agave to be cooked and its juice fermented and distilled for the magical transformation into tequila.

**pulque** (pull-keh) — a viscous, milky-looking liquid, fermented but not distilled, that has been a local drink from Mexico's pre-Hispanic days and is still quite popular in parts of Mexico; it can be made from several species of the agave but never from the tequila agave.

**tequila** (teh-kee-lah) — the distilled spirit of the fermented juice of a specific agave plant, called Tequilana Weber Amaryllidacaeae, Blue Variety, which has been found to grow and mature successfully only in the state of Jalisco and parts of Michoacan and Nayarit in Mexico (which area incudes Guadalajara and the town of Tequila).

**tequilero** (masc) or *tequilera* (fem.) (teh-kee-ler-o, a) — a producer or associate in the production of tequila.

# Part 2:

# The Tequila Gourmet

Tequila's character is two things at once: it is chameleonlike, and thus can absorb and heighten the flavors of a wide variety of potables and edibles; but, at the same time, the potion also maintains its integrity—casting its own unique essence over any food or drink companion.

The spirit of tequila invites the creation of your own power mixture. To stimulate your imagination and appetite, here are more than 100 drink and food ideas, with the continuing story of tequila interspersed in anecdotes along the way. The food category follows the drinks, divided for easy reference into four groups: straights and chasers, lowballs and high-balls, cocktails, and punchy mixtures.

Every recipe creates a taste sensation and will have you habitually offering the spirited toast traditional in the land of tequila: Salud, dinero, y amor—tiempo gustarlos! (Health, money, and love—and the time to enjoy them!)

# 1

# Straights and Chasers

Any beverage served "neat" means, by definition, that it is free of admixture or dilution. A tequila connoisseur's delight, drinking it neat is as easy as I, II, III.

## Tequila Neat I

Traditionally, tequila is downed with ritual. Instructions seem to vary as much as the hearty souls who endorse the method, but one thing is certain—the kinetics seem to be part of the kick.

In Mexico, the connoisseur will moisten the base of his thumb and sprinkle salt on it. He takes a small glass of tequila between his thumb and forefinger, while holding a wedge of lime between his forefinger and middle finger. Then he licks the salt, downs the tequila and bites into the lime, all in one resolute gesture.

*(From Montezuma Tequila, Barton Brands Ltd.)*

## Tequila Neat II

Using the left hand only, hold a shot glass of tequila with the thumb and forefinger; with a wedge of limon (the unique Mexican lime/lemon—in the United States use either) squeeze a few drops of juice between the knuckles of the forefinger and middle finger; then put a few grains of coarse salt in the small hollow of the wrist. Now, quickly and with a raise of the left hand—lick limon, drink tequila, lick salt.

With a little practice you can pull off this three-step ritual with the apparent abandon of a native Mexican.

*(From Juan Orendain, Guadalajara, Mexico)*

# Tequila on the Rocks

1 jigger tequila
Ice cubes
Maggi sauce or Bovril

Pour tequila over ice, add dash of Maggi or Bovril, and drink up. (1 serving)

(From Tequila Eucario Gonzalez, Mexico)

# Head Shrinker

2 ounces orange juice
¾ ounce lemon juice
¾ ounce grenadine
10–12 drops Tabasco
½ teaspoon salt
Cracked ice
1 ½ ounces tequila

Shake all ingredients — except tequila — with cracked ice. Strain into 6-ounce sour glass. Toss off tequila straight, preferably nicely chilled, then down the chaser. (1 serving)

(*From* San Diego *magazine, July, 1969*)

# Monja Loca (Crazy Nun)

Half-part tequila
Half-part anisette
Crushed ice

Pour both ingredients over the ice. (1 serving)

(*From* A Guide to Tequila, Mezcal and Pulque, *by Virginia B. de Barrios*)

# The Sangrita Debate

Pepe Arreola Santiago, designer and operator of one of the best Mexican restaurants, Tlaquepaque (pronounced t'lakee-pakee), in Acapulco, serves up the original Sangrita, the fabulous chili and orange juice tequila chaser, as taught him by the drink's creator, the Widow Sanchez, when he worked for her in her restaurant in Chapala.

Sangrita's inventor, the Widow Sanchez—Guadalupe—is retired now. She still lives in Chapala, tequila country, where she and husband Jose had a bar in the twenties and thirties. Here they poured the local spirit, el tequila, and sold postcards, cameras, film, and assorted tourist needs. In those days Lake Chapala was a favorite Mexican resort and theirs was the only decent bar in town. After Jose died, Guadalupe opened a restaurant still operated today by son Gustavo. Naturally, the house drink is Tequila con Sangrita—as chaser, cocktail, or highball.

On the Widow Sanchez's authority, Pepe vehemently declares that the original Sangrita formula does not call for any tomato juice, a standard ingredient in most commercial mixes and recipes. Pepe's is a mixture of orange juice—made from tart Mexican oranges; lots of Bufalo salsa picante—the red sauce ubiquitous in Mexico and now becoming available in the United States; salt; Worcestershire; and grenadine. Beyond these general ingredients, Pepe will not divulge the specifics of his inherited formula, thus the absence of his Sangrita recipe in this collection.

# Sangrita

In Mexico, Sangrita (spiced tomato, orange, and lime juices) and tequila are served separately. The practice is to sip the tequila, then take a little Sangrita as a chaser. It's a sure cure for morning sickness.

8 ounces tomato juice
4 ounces orange juice
¾ ounce lime juice
¾ ounce Worcestershire
½ teaspoon Tabasco
½ teaspoon finely minced onion
½ teaspoon salt
Ice
2 jiggers tequila

Shake ingredients — except tequila — with ice cubes and strain into small pitcher, then pour into two tumblers. Serve individual jiggers of tequila and sip alternately with Sangrita. (2 servings)

(*From* San Diego *magazine, July, 1969*)

# S O B

This is the fanciest way to drink tequila and still be a purist. Fill a long-stemmed shot glass with tequila and place it in a metal saucer containing brandy. Peel a lemon wheel. Soak it in Galliano, cover it with sugar, and place it on top of the shot glass. Light the brandy. After the juice from the sugared lemon has dripped into the shot glass (and the flame has died down), lift the lemon wheel off the glass, take a swig of the tequila, then immediately bite the lemon. (1 serving)

(*From* Texas Monthly, *September, 1975*)

# Submarine

1 ounce tequila
1 glass beer,  ¾ full

Pour tequila into beer. (1 serving)

(*From Su Casa Restaurant, Chicago*)

# Submarino

Drop 1 shot glass filled with tequila into a large mug filled with beer. Please note that the shot glass as well as the tequila in it are dropped into the mug of beer. Natives claim the addition of the tequila lightens the taste of the beer. (1 serving)

This drinking exercise is also called Vaca Parida (Pregnant Cow).

(*From Juan Orendain, Guadalajara, Mexico*)

# Submarino with a Touch of Style

A variation of the submarino is a drink enjoyed by Teddy Stauffer in Acapulco. His own description: "The submarino has always been my drink in all the years I have lived in Mexico. By now most clubs and restaurants know the ceremony so that as soon as I sit down they bring me a shot of tequila, a champagne glass and bottle of beer in a champagne cooler. So I take my tequila, and then take my champagne glass and pour in the beer, and that is my chaser. The standard submarino is when you drop the tequila glass in the beer, but mine drops in the stomach, there it meets, not in the glass."

# The Blue Horseshoe

In tequila country the blue horseshoe is lady luck mounted on the label of every bottle of Tequila Herradura (herradura meaning horseshoe).

Tequilera Gabriela de la Peña de Romo reigns over the Hacienda de San Jose del Refugio in Amatitan, a tiny town immediately east of the town of Tequila. The best way to describe Gabriela's dedication is to liken her to French champagne country's Madame Bollinger who in her eighties still bicycled through her vineyards and directed the vendange (the critical moment of picking). Gabriela inherited her unique property from her mother and, like her mother, she is the active, operating owner of the Herradura agave plantation and distillery. No batch of tequila is bottled until a sample has been personally tasted and approved by Gabriela, a practice also followed by her mother.

The approach to the Herradura hacienda, founded in 1870, is reminiscent of the gateway and colonnade of trees lining the entry to the great wine chateau of Margaux in Bordeaux, France. Inside the grounds, beautiful, terraced, formal gardens punctuated with ancient and colonial sculptures weave around the workers' houses, the great house, the family chapel, corrals, and the numerous other buildings.

The Herradura hacienda encloses one of the finest museums of tequila history. Here the tequila-making process of the past century returns to life. On display to stir the viewer's imagination are the "dungeon" of ovens, the great stone wheels once drawn by oxen to crush the cooked agave hearts, the deep, narrow stone reservoir for water, and the charming old copper pot stills with arms outstretched.

# Añejo en Rocas
## (Aged tequila on the rocks)

2 ounces añejo tequila
Water as desired
Ice cubes
Large twist of orange peel

Pour tequila and water into an old-fashioned glass filled with ice cubes. Top with orange peel, stir, and serve. (1 serving)

*(Ing. Carlos Rosales, Tequila Rosales, Mexico)*

# La Cura, or
# For the Morning After

1 jigger tequila

Pour it and drink it, that's all. (1 serving)

*(From Alejandro Prieto de Sierra, Mexico City)*

# 2

# Lowballs and Highballs

## Drink Tequila and Feed the Starving

*While Americans are being urged to eat less grain-fed meats in order to free grain for the world's hungry millions, a companion grain-saving measure has been suggested that hits at another American institution—alcohol.*

*The idea is that a cutback in the billions of gallons of grain-based alcoholic beverages—beer and most hard liquors (beer, bourbon, Scotch and Irish whiskey, rye and Canadian whiskey, gin, and vodka)—that Americans drink each year could theoretically provide food for millions of people.*

*While the total of 4.1 million tons of grain used in 1973 to produce alcoholic beverages represents only 1.6 percent of the total food and feed grains grown in the United States last year, it is still enough food for one year for more than 20 million people living on a minimal adequate diet.*

*Looking at American consumption of alcoholic beverages—402 million gallons of distilled spirits and 4.2 billion gallons of beer last year—it might be said that Americans annually drink up the amount of grain that could feed 25 million people a year.*

(New York Times
December 11, 1974)

*Author's note:* The moral of this story? Leave more grain for food. Tequila is made from the heart of the agave, not from grain — join the tequila movement.

# Tequila Buttermilk

1 ½ ounces tequila
1 bottle lemon/lime soft drink
Cracked ice

Mix all ingredients in blender. Serve garnished with lemon or lime wedge. (1 serving)

*(From Montezuma Tequila, Barton Brands Ltd.)*

# Planters Punch

Juice of ½ lemon
Juice of ½ orange
1 ½ ounces tequila
1 ½ ounces grenadine
Cracked ice

Shake all ingredients together and pour into tall glass filled with the ice. Stir. Decorate with fruit and serve with straws. (1 serving)

*(From Tequila San Matias, Mexico)*

# Blizzard

1 ½ ounces tequila
Ice
Fresca
Wedge of lemon or lime

Put tequila into a tall glass filled with ice. Fill glass with Fresca and add a wedge of lemon or lime. Stir. (1 serving)

*(From Jose Cuervo Tequila, Heublein, Inc.)*

# Tequila Fizz

2 ounces tequila
Juice of ½ fresh lime (save the shell )
½ teaspoon sugar
2 dashes orange bitters
Ice
Club soda

Stir the first 4 ingredients in a tall glass filled with ice. Fill with club soda. Garnish with the lime shell. (1 serving)

*(From Montezuma Tequila, Barton Brands Ltd.)*

# C. C.

1 ½ ounces tequila
1 ounce lemon juice
1 teaspoon sugar
Ice
Coffee (hot and very strong)

Add tequila, lemon juice, and sugar to a 10-ounce highball glass. Fill glass nearly to its rim with crushed ice. Pour coffee over the ice and stir to mix. Serve. (1 serving)

*(From* San Diego *magazine, July, 1969)*

# Pancho Villa

All it takes is a few sips of any tequila concoction to stir up memories of Mexico's most memorable hero. The spirit of Pancho Villa, a legendary aficionado of tequila, lives on in Mexico and in the U.S. Southwest, as evidenced by the 1973 Los Angeles Press Club luncheon honoring the surviving Mrs. Pancho Villa. Whether or not Pancho Villa was a hero depends upon whom you talk to, especially in Mexico. He was a bandit, both in Mexico and on the U.S. southern border, but the intrigue and fascination was in his strategy; he was never captured. He finally did retire in Chihuahua when some property was offered to him, but this did not protect him from a violent death. He was shot and killed in 1915 while riding in a car.

On the subject of rough-and-ready heroes, tequila producers know who the best purveyors of their spirit are. If it's good enough for Zorro and the Cisco Kid, it's a winner, Seagram Distillers must have reasoned. They recently introduced a new brand of tequila, El Charro, and with a "Fiesta of the Flicks," a 50¢ triple-feature film festival, who could resist ordering up when Zorro and the Kid swig the fiery stuff—El Charro—edited into scenes in the thirty-year-old flick? Charles E. Bird, Inc., Hollywood youth-marketing consultants, thought up the fiesta, which also includes a nostalgic newsreel.

So, think of the black-masked man and the mustachioed hero the next time you saunter into a bar and ask for a shot of the strong stuff.

# Can-Can

1 jigger tequila
½ jigger French vermouth
2 jiggers grapefruit juice
1 teaspoon sugar
Ice
Orange twist

Shake ingredients together over ice and serve with the twist. (1 serving)

*(From Tequila Eucario Gonzalez, Mexico)*

# Piña

1 ½ ounces tequila
3 ounces pineapple juice
1 ounce lime juice
Sugar to taste

Shake all ingredients together. Serve on the rocks in a tall glass. (1 serving)

*(From Montezuma Tequila, Barton Brands Ltd.)*

## Azteca de Oro (Golden Aztec)

1 ounce aged (or gold) tequila
⅓ ounce Damiana liqueur
1 ounce orange juice
Ice
Orange peel

Pour the tequila, liqueur, and juice over 3 cubes of ice in an old-fashioned glass. Garnish with twist of orange peel. (1 serving)

*(From Tequila Sauza, Mexico)*

## Bertha

1 jigger honey
1 jigger lime juice
2 jiggers white tequila
Ice
Soda water
Fresh lime

Place first three ingredients into mixing glass, mix well, and pour into tall glass with 3 ice cubes. Fill to top with soda water. Mix and add a slice of lime. Serve with long straws. (1 serving)

*(From Vernon O. Underwood, Sr., Young's Market Co., who obtained it from Bertha's Restaurant, in Taxco, Mexico)*

# Sing Tequila

But for the grace of fate, we would've been humming "Tecate" instead of "Tequila." The two-million-record seller of the sixties, "Tequila," recorded by such stars as Perez Prado, Xavier Cugat, and Wes Montgomery, came about by accident. Vern Underwood, liquor distributor and benefactor of tequila, brought the first bottle of Jose Cuervo into the United States in 1942. His advertising agent happened onto a group cutting a record and deciphered the word Tecate, which is the name of a small Mexican border town whose only claim to fame is the Tecate beer manufactured there. Perhaps prescient of the tequila trend, he suggested the group change one word of their song — tecate — and make it tequila. The rest is music history. Tequila music makes appearances, directly and indirectly, at the Newport Jazz Festival, held in New York City since 1972. Every jazz man has his favorite arrangement of "Tequila," and whenever Harry James and Sy Oliver swing into "Sunrise Serenade" and "The World Is Waiting for the Sunrise," tequila lovers can't be far behind.

If tequila mixes with jazz, it surely mixes with rock. The flamboyant Mick Jagger and the Rolling Stones swear by the inspiration in a Sunrise, the Eagles make a hit with "Just Another Tequila Sunrise," and a record cover for David Clayton-Thomas of Blood, Sweat and Tears proudly displays tequila, the symbol of a generation.

# Bertita's Special

2 ounces tequila
Juice of 1 lime
1 teaspoon sugar
2 dashes of orange bitters
Cracked ice
Soda water

Combine first four ingredients with cracked ice in a shaker and shake vigorously. Strain into a Tom Collins glass and fill with chilled soda water. (1 serving)

Variation: Add the white of an egg to the shaker mixture and shake vigorously. This turns a Bertita's Special into a Taxco Fizz.

(*From* The Complete Book of Mexican Cooking, *by Elisabeth Lambert Ortiz*)

# Hot Shot

1 cube beef bouillon
Boiling water
1 ½ ounces tequila
Seasoning, as desired

Dissolve the cube of beef bouillon in a mug of boiling water. Add the tequila and season to taste. (1 serving)

(*From Montezuma Tequila, Barton Brands Ltd.*)

# Bloody Bull

1 ½ ounces tequila
1 ½ ounces tomato juice
1 ½ ounces canned beef bouillon, undiluted
Ice
Pepper and Worcestershire sauce, to taste
Thick slice lemon

Pour tequila, juice, and bouillon over ice in a tall glass. Add seasonings, as desired. Stir to chill. Drop in lemon slice and serve. (1 serving)

Variation: With 3 ounces of beef bouillon, instead of half bouillon-half tomato juice, a Bloody Bull becomes a Plain Bull.

*(From Ole Tequila, Schenley Imports Co.)*

# Bloody Maria

1 ½ ounces white tequila
3 ounces tomato juice
½ ounce lemon juice
1 dash Worcestershire sauce
Salt and pepper to taste
Ice

Shake all ingredients with ice and strain into glass. (1 serving)

*(From Tequila Sauza, National Distillers Products Co.)*

# Bloody Mary

1 ½ ounces tequila
3 ounces tomato juice
Salt and pepper to taste
½ ounce lemon juice
Dash Worcestershire sauce
Dash hot sauce
Cracked ice

Shake all ingredients with cracked ice; strain into a 6-ounce glass. (1 serving)

*(From Jose Cuervo Tequila, Heublein, Inc.)*

# Tequila Maria

Generous pinch of white pepper
Generous pinch of celery salt
Bottled hot pepper sauce, to taste
Generous dash of Worcestershire sauce
Generous pinch of oregano or tarragon or dill
Juice of ¼ fresh lime
½ teaspoon fresh, grated horseradish
2 ounces tequila
8 ounces tomato juice
Cracked ice

Stir all ingredients briskly with cracked ice and serve in a chilled, 14-ounce double-old-fashioned glass. (1 serving)

*(From John J. Poister,* Venture *Magazine)*

# Beetleboards

A fiesta of flicks may be one thing, but a Beetleboard army is another . . . another promotion by Schenley Ole Tequila. Anyone who wants to shout about tequila from his or her Volkswagen rooftop can have a Schenley Ole tequila ad painted all over their bugs. To date, Ole is riding the backs of VWs in California, Florida, Massachusetts, New Jersey, Arizona, and Mexico City.

# Brave Bull

1½ ounces tequila
Ice
1½ ounces Kahlua
Lemon twist

Pour tequila into an old-fashioned glass filled with ice. Then add Kahlua and lemon twist. Stir. (1 serving)

*(From Jose Cuervo Tequila, Heublein, Inc.)*

# Snowblast

1½ ounces tequila
12 ounces ice
Fresca

Take 1½ ounces of tequila and set it aside. Or drink it, and set another 1½ ounces aside. Then take the ice, fill a glass with it, pour in the tequila, and fill up the glass with Fresca. (1 serving)

*(From Montezuma Tequila, Barton Brands Ltd.)*

# Cactus Banger

1 ounce Neapolitan liqueur
1 ounce tequila
Ice
Squirt
Fresh lime

Mix liqueur and tequila in a tall glass. Add ice and Squirt to fill and garnish with a slice of lime. (1 serving)

# Tijuana Taxi

Ice
1½ ounces white or gold tequila
Squeeze of lime
Dr. Pepper

Fill a highball glass with ice. Add tequila and lime. Fill glass with Dr. Pepper and serve. (1 serving)

*(From El Charro Tequila, Seagram Distillers Corp.)*

# Cafe Tequila

Crushed ice
1½ ounces tequila
1 teaspoon sugar
½ ounce lemon juice
Double-strength coffee

Fill a highball glass to the rim with ice. Add tequila, sugar, and lemon juice. Pour coffee over the ice to top of glass. (1 serving)

*(From Jose Cuervo Tequila, Heublein, Inc.)*

# A Bottle of
# "Elizabeth Taylor Tequila," Please

Some say that the picture of the Viuda de Romero gracing the label of every bottle of Mexico's third largest brand of tequila of the same name is a look-alike for the beauteous green-eyed raven-haired Ms. Taylor. The beauty of the tequila label and her portrait are vintage 19th century, from one of the earliest chartered tequila producers. And the widow (viuda) Romero, also beautiful, green-eyed, and raven-haired, actually did distill el tequila in those rough and hairy times.

The story goes that the founder of Tequila Romero, one Francisco Romero, married one of the belles of Jalisco state's high aristocracy. Although in those times it was very unusual that a woman worked in a business instead of just being the lady of the house, Senora Romero did work beside her husband in the distillation of el tequila for many years in addition to leading a very social life and hostessing many of the grand parties of the time. When her husband Francisco died, she continued serving el tequila, renamed her product for herself (Tequila Viuda de Romero), and had the drawing of her likeness made for the label.

Sadly, this magnificent pioneer couple had no heirs, and when the widow died, the mark (name and label of Tequila Viuda de Romero) was sold to Eucario Gonzalez. He subsequently gave it to his son, the contemporary, handsome and dashing Joaquin Gonzalez Chavez, who continues the distillation of the Tequila Viuda de Romero today—in the tradition of the original founders—alongside another beautiful, green-eyed, raven-haired woman, his daughter, Beatriz.

The tequila in the green bottle, the spirit of green-eyed, raven-haired women—Viuda de Romero, Elizabeth Taylor, and Beatriz Gonzalez de Cue.

# Golden Knife

2 ounces gold tequila
1½ ounces lemon juice
2 teaspoons sugar
2 dashes bitters
1 egg
Ice
Iced club soda
Salt

Blend first five ingredients with ice. Strain mixture into 14-ounce glass with more ice. Fill with soda and sprinkle with salt. (1 serving)

*(From Montezuma Tequila, Barton Brands Ltd.)*

# ¡Caramba!

1½ ounces white tequila
3 ounces grapefruit juice
1 tablespoon sugar
Cracked ice
Club soda

Shake together all ingredients, except club soda, with ice. Add club soda and serve in highball glass. (1 serving)

*(From Jose Cuervo Tequila, Heublein, Inc.)*

# Changuirongo

1 ½ ounces tequila
Ice
Orange Crush
Wedge of lemon or lime

Add tequila to a highball glass filled with ice and fill with Orange Crush. Garnish with wedge of lemon or lime. (1 serving)

According to Virginia de Barrios in *A Guide to Tequila, Mezcal and Pulque,* the changuirongo is a combination of tequila and any handy carbonated soft drink.

*(From Jose [Pepe] Santiago Areola, Tlaquepaque Restaurant, Acapulco, Mexico)*

# Chato

(Chato has two meanings: Pug nose or small drink.)
1 jigger gin
½ jigger vermouth
½ jigger tequila

Combine all ingredients in small glass and drink up. (1 serving)

*(From Juan Orendain, Guadalajara, Mexico)*

## Coctel (Cocktail) Hotel Plaza del Sol

½ ounce tequila
¼ ounce mandarine liqueur
½ ounce lemon or lime juice
½ ounce orange juice
¼ ounce tangerine liqueur
½ ounce grenadine
Ice

Mix all ingredients together in a tall glass filled with ice. (1 serving)

The Guadalajara *Colony Reporter* notes: "The color of the Coctel Hotel Plaza del Sol wouldn't even bear mentioning except to note that it must match exactly the red-orange of the stripes on the lounge napkins. The quality, however, especially after such an apparently effortless preparation by Manuel, sends the eyebrows shooting sunwards in rapturous surprise. 'The Coctel Hotel Plaza del Sol,' Manuel quietly proclaims after the first splendid sip, and takes a small but rightful bow. Manuel says that the bar won't change its specialty until the sun changes color."

(*From Manuel, at Hotel Plaza del Sol, Guadalajara, Mexico*)

## Ole Cocktail

1 ½ ounces tequila
Ice
Pineapple-grapefruit juice, chilled

Pour tequila over ice cubes in a tall glass. Fill with pineapple-grapefruit juice. (1 serving)

(*From Ole Tequila, Schenley Imports Co.*)

# Mariachi

Born in the land of the blue agave, where would mariachi, a Mexican street band and the music it plays, be without tequila? Such compadres, are they not? In Guadalajara's La Plaza del Mariachi one finds the heart of Mexican music, and almost equal in spirit is the Plaza Garibaldi, in Mexico City.

Maybe the best time for mariachi follows the late-hour Mexican dinner, around 11 P.M. It begins as a noisy, bustling scene: dozens of colorfully costumed combos stand in clusters, all playing different songs and competing for attention.

A mariachi group usually consists of nine members: four with violins, two guitarists, one with a guitarron, or bass guitar, and two with trumpets. They move freely and are not assigned to any particular bar or spot in the open plaza. Some wait curbside for random "bookings"—people who drive up and hire them to serenade parties and gatherings in their private homes.

A true mariachi evening lasts for hours as patrons sit in the plaza bars sipping tequila straight (or with chaser) and listening to a spirited repertoire voicing the many moods of tequila land. Perhaps "Las Olas," "Cielito Lindo," "Guadalajara," "La Adelita," or maybe "Jesusita en Chihuahua." Almost always someone can be counted on to rise from the audience and sing with the strolling musicians.

Mariachi is unique. Nowhere else in the world has such a style of music risen from one spot and retained its identity with its environment, even though it takes many forms—sounding like everything from waltzes to ballads to polkas.

The most widely agreed upon origin of the word "mariachi," suggests that it is a permutation of the French word *mariage* which means wedding. It is believed that these musical groups escorted the wedding parties of French settlers who were scattered in the state of Jalisco after the fall of Emperor Maximilian, during the 1860s. The mariachi definitely originated in tequila territory, but no one knows exactly when they first appeared. Once known as big harp bands, the original instruments used by these strolling minstrels were the harp, guitar, violin, guitarron, and the military drum, the latter being excluded sometime around the late 1800s. Trumpets had been added by the forties.

## Tequila 'N Cola

Juice and rind of ½ lemon
Ice
1 ounce white tequila
Cola

Squeeze lemon over ice cubes in a tall glass. Add rind. Pour in tequila. Fill with cola. (1 serving)

*(From Tequila Sauza, National Distillers Products Co.)*

## Tequila Collins

1 teaspoon of sugar
½ ounce lemon juice
Ice
1 ounce white tequila
Soda water
Maraschino cherry (optional)

In tall glass, dissolve sugar in juice. Add ice and tequila. Fill with soda water and stir. Garnish with cherry. (1 serving)

*(From Tequila Sauza, National Distillers Products Co.)*

# Tequila Comfort

1 ½ ounces tequila
1 ½ ounces Southern Comfort cordial or liqueur
Ice
Lemon twist

Add the tequila and Southern Comfort to an old-fashioned glass filled with ice. Garnish with twist of lemon. (1 serving)

*(From Jose Cuervo Tequila, Heublein, Inc.)*

# El Diablo

1 ½ ounces tequila
½ ounce Crème de Cassis
½ ounce lime juice
Ice
Ginger ale
Fresh lime (optional)

Pour ingredients over ice cubes in 10-ounce highball glass. Fill glass with ginger ale. Garnish with lime slice. (1 serving)

*(From* San Diego *magazine, July, 1969)*

# Taking a Bead on the Crow

It seems that for many, many years the Cuervo family believed that Tequila Cuervo, S.A. was founded in the year 1800 and, therefore, applied the name "Cuervo 1800" to that aged tequila which was strictly private family stock (until 1974). It was only recently that some old family records were found which revealed that Cuervo was, in fact, established in 1795! There are no plans to change the label of aged Cuervo to "Cuervo 1795".

# Tequila Fizz

2 ounces tequila
1½ ounces lemon juice
2 teaspoons sugar
2 dashes Angostura bitters
1 small egg
Ice
Club soda (chilled)
Salt

Shake or mix in blender tequila, lemon juice, sugar, bitters, egg, and ice. Strain into tall, 14-ounce glass half-filled with ice. Fill glass with soda, stir, and sprinkle very lightly with salt. (1 serving)

*(From Jose Cuervo Tequila, Heublein, Inc.)*

# Freddy Fudpucker
## or
# Grande Tequila Wallbanger(?)

Ice
1½ ounces tequila
1 ounce Liquore Martinoni
Orange juice to fill
Orange slice (fresh)

Pre-chill a tall glass. Add ice cubes and fill with ingredients. Top with a slice of orange. Stir gently. (1 serving)

*(From Pancho Villa Tequila, E. Martinoni Co.)*

# Tequila Gimlet

Cracked ice
1½ ounces tequila
Juice of 1 lime

In an old-fashioned glass, combine tequila and juice with ice. Stir and serve. (1 serving)

*(From Pancho Villa Tequila, E. Martinoni Co.)*

# Mexicola

Ice
1½ ounces tequila
Cola
Twist of lemon

Place ice cubes in 10-ounce highball glass. Add tequila and fill glass with a cola. Add lemon twist. (1 serving)

*(From San Diego magazine, July, 1969)*

# Mountain Mover

1½ ounces tequila
1½ teaspoons sugar
Juice of ½ lemon or lime
Dash red wine
Cracked ice
Twist of lemon

Combine first four ingredients in a bar glass and pour into tall glass prepared with cracked ice. Garnish with lemon peel twist. (1 serving)

*(From Beverage Media)*

# New Life

1 lump sugar
5 drops angostura bitters
Cracked ice
1½ ounces white tequila
Twist of lemon

Muddle sugar and bitters in an old-fashioned glass. Fill glass with cracked ice. Add tequila and twist of lemon peel. Stir well and serve. (1 serving)

*(From Tequila Sauza, National Distillers Products Co.)*

# New York

2 parts gold tequila
1 part sweet vermouth
Squeeze of lime
Maraschino cherry
Fresh orange wedge

Mix and serve tequila, vermouth, and lime on the rocks in an old-fashioned glass. Garnish with cherry and wedge of orange. (1 serving)

*(From Jose Cuervo Tequila, Heublein, Inc.)*

# Pandora's Box

1½ ounces white tequila
3½ ounces pineapple juice
½ ounce triple sec
Ice

Stir all ingredients with ice and serve. (1 serving)

*(From Don Emilio Tequila, Bacardi Imports, Inc.)*

# Pepe Cuervo
## (Pepe is the nickname for Jose)

3 ice cubes
1½ ounces aged tequila
Few drops of lemon juice
Cold sangria (red wine mix)

Put the ice, tequila, and lemon juice into a tall glass. Fill with Sangria and serve. (1 serving)

*(From Tequila Cuervo, Mexico)*

# Petroleo

1½ ounces tequila
1 teaspoon Maggi sauce
1 teaspoon lemon juice
Ice

Pour ingredients over ice in an old-fashioned glass. (1 serving)

*(From Senora Sara Lopez Figueroa de Morales, Mexico City)*

# Mexican Jive

When a couple dances the Jarabe Tapatio, they are dancing the spirit of tequila, to the accompaniment of mariachi. This most famous of the regional Mexican dances is performed one couple at a time. The woman wears a dress of the Mexican colonial period, and the man sports the fancy gear and great hat of the charro (the Mexican gentleman-cowboy). During the fiery spirit of the dance, el charro throws his hat to the ground.

Other dances reflect the opposing forces of Mexico's history—the spirit of pre-Columbian tribes and the powerful force of the Spanish conquerors.

The dance of Conquest is done all over the state of Jalisco, and represents, as the name indicates, Mexico's captivity under foreign rulers. It is primarily danced at religious festivities today, and especially to solemnize the feast.

The most vigorous dance of the entire tequila region is the Dance of the Rattlers, the name derived from the ancient Aztec rattles used. The courage of the Mexican people and the pageantry of their heritage spring vibrantly to life in its tones and rhythm.

A pantomimic dance created by the conquerors during the colonial period, the Dance of the Tastoanes, shows the strong artistic characteristics of the original native inhabitants of tequila land. It recreates a theme of European conquest, where religious characters of early Christianity take part, along with pagans of Greek mythology, opposed by the Indians, rebels of the European conquest.

The first spot in North America to go go-go was Teddy, "Mr. Acapulco," Stauffer's place in Acapulco. Even before Joey Dees' famous Peppermint Lounge opened in New York, everybody from the Kennedy clan to Linda Bird Johnson and George Hamilton was packing Teddy's "Tequila A-Go-Go" to jumping room only. "We had every kind of tequila and every kind of drink," says Teddy.

## Rattler

1 ½ ounces gold or white tequila
2-3 ounces grapefruit juice
Splash of triple sec
Juice of ¼ lime (save the wedge)
Ice

Mix ingredients in a tall glass filled with the ice. Add wedge of lime. (1 serving)

*(From Olmeca Tequila, General Wine and Spirits Co.)*

## Gotcha!

1 ½ ounces tequila
Cracked ice
1 teaspoon sugar
½ ounce grenadine
½ ounce lime juice
Tonic water
Wedge of lime

Pour tequila into highball glass, over cracked ice. Add sugar, grenadine, and lime juice. Fill with tonic water and stir. Garnish with lime wedge. (1 serving)

*(From Pancho Villa Tequila, E. Martinoni Co.,*
*and Robert E. Petrone, Knoxville, Tennessee)*

# Jarana
## (Merrymaker — pronounced "harana")

2 ounces white tequila
3 teaspoons sugar or syrup
Ice
Pineapple juice

Mix tequila and sugar (or syrup) in highball glass. Add cubes of ice and fill with pineapple juice. (1 serving)

*(From Tequila Sauza, Mexico)*

# Hammer

1 ½ ounces tequila
Orange juice
Ice
Fresh orange slice (optional)

Pour tequila and orange juice over ice in an 8-ounce highball glass and stir. Serve garnished with a half slice of orange, if you like. (1 serving)

*(From Ole Tequila, Schenley Imports Co.)*

# Hula Hula

1 part tequila
2 parts Hawaiian punch

Mix and serve in highball glass over ice. (1 serving)

*(From Tequila Eucario Gonzalez, Mexico)*

## Sauza Highball

1 ½ ounces Tequila Sauza Conmemorativo (aged)
Ice
Club soda or water

Pour tequila over ice in highball glass. Fill with soda or water and stir. (1 serving)

*(From Tequila Sauza, National Distillers Products Co.)*

## Tequila Lima

Ice
1 ½ ounces tequila
1 ounce Rose's lime juice
Wedge of lime

In a highball glass put 3 cubes of ice, the tequila, and lime juice. Stir well. Garnish with lime. (1 serving)

*(From Club de Industriales, Mexico City)*

## Salta Para Atras
## (Kick from Behind)

1 ounce tequila
½ ounce gin
1 ½ ounces prepared Sangrita *
Ice

Stir ingredients into a martini or old-fashioned glass. (1 serving)

*See* index.                     *(From Juan Orendain, Guadalajara, Mexico)*

# Tequila Rainbow

½ ounce grenadine
1 ounce lemon juice
1 ounce pineapple juice
1 ounce orange juice
2 ounces white tequila
Juice of ½ lime
Ginger ale

Pour first six ingredients into a tall glass and fill with ginger ale. (1 serving)

*(From Tequila Sauza, National Distillers Products Co.)*

# Rocio (Dew)

Shaved ice
1½ ounces white tequila
Juice of ½ lemon
Twist of lemon

Fill an old-fashioned glass with the shaved ice and pour the tequila and the lemon juice over it. Add a small twist of lemon peel. (1 serving)

*(From Tequila Sauza, Mexico)*

# Tequila and Soda

Aged tequila (añejo) to taste
3 ice cubes
Soda water

Into a tall glass, pour the añejo over the ice cubes. Fill to top
with soda water. (1 serving)

*(From Tequila Cuervo, Mexico)*

# Spanish Fly

1 part tequila
1 part Cuarenta y Tres liqueur
Crushed ice
Ground cinnamon
Cinnamon stick

Pour tequila and the liqueur over crushed ice in a lowball
glass. Sprinkle with cinnamon and garnish with a cinnamon
stick. (1 serving)

*(From Schenley World T. & I. Co.)*

# Skip, Run, and Go Naked

A short beer
A double shot of tequila
Dash of bitters

Mix and drink. (1 serving)

*(From Shawn Christie, Merchant's Cafe, Seattle; and Pancho Villa Tequila, E. Martinoni Co.)*

# Spray

Ice cubes
1½ ounces tequila
½ ounce Strega liqueur
2 ounces cranberry juice cocktail
1 ounce pineapple juice

Fill a tall glass with ice cubes. Add all remaining ingredients and stir. (1 serving)

(*From Ole Tequila, Schenley Imports Co.*)

# The Sun Also Rises

Sy Feit, Jos. E. Seagram Sons' tequila expert, contends the Sunrise is a permutation of the screwdriver: "Some smart aleck in California took a screwdriver and made it with *tequila*. Great! Then another smart guy added grenadine. Great! Then another wise guy said, 'Gee, it looks like a sunrise!'"

Mexophile Mac Wasson (Sauza's man) pegs the origin of the sunrise at least back to 1940, recalling, "It was my father's favorite drink. I remember going to Ensenada with my father and mother and sister back then, and I also remember mother being angry with my father because he was drinking too many Tequila Sunrises on the way down there; he loved that drink."

Recalls Vernon Underwood, Sr., of Young's Market Co., "I think it is true that the Sunrise originated in the West, in Mexico, at Agua Caliente, during prohibition days when Caliente was the playground for the so-called 'smart set' of Southern California, and the racetrack was going full blast.

"Then the prescription was somewhat different from what it is today and was used for hangovers. Everyone would line up at the bar the morning after and drink sunrises," says Vern, who was one of the participants. "That is how the name began—you could greet the new day after imbibing the sunrise." Vern generously shared the formula for this restorative in his tequila recipe booklet that Jose Cuervo distributed after prohibition, but "we couldn't put in any literature that it was for hangovers; the government wouldn't allow it."

Anyway here is a Cuervo "Original" and "Classical," guaranteed to help your sunrise—either as it ends your evening or begins your morning.

## Sunrise (Original)

1½ ounces tequila
½ ounce lime juice
3 ounces orange juice
½ ounce grenadine
Ice
Fresh lime

Shake ingredients together. Serve in tall glass of ice, garnished with a wedge or slice of lime. (1 serving)

*(From Jose Cuervo Tequila, Heublein, Inc.)*

## Sunrise (Classical)

2 ounces tequila
½ ounce lime juice
½ ounce orange curacao
1 teaspoon crème de cassis
Ice
Club soda
Slice of lime

Vigorously shake tequila, lime juice, curacao, and crème de cassis with ice. Strain into a tall, 14-ounce glass half-filled with ice. Fill to top with soda and stir. Garnish with lime. (1 serving)

*(From Jose Cuervo Tequila, Heublein, Inc.)*

# Teul

Ice
1 ounce tequila
1 ounce Southern Comfort
Orange juice to fill

In a highball glass filled with ice cubes add all ingredients and stir. (1 serving)

*(From Pancho Villa Tequila, E. Martinoni Co.)*

# T'N'T

1 ½ ounces tequila
Cracked ice
Tonic water
Lime wedge

Pour tequila over the ice in a highball glass. Fill with tonic. Stir and garnish with lime. (1 serving)

*(From Jose Cuervo Tequila, Heublein, Inc.)*

# 3

# Cocktails

## The Hatfields and the McCoys of Tequila

*The biggest producers of el tequila, Cuervo and Sauza, are engaged in an all-out war, both aiming for the largest share of the tequila market. [At this writing, it's Sauza's point in Mexico and Cuervo's in the United States.] Today's rivalry is a friendly one, but the Cuervo and Sauza families were not always so amiable. The feuding of the rival clans often was backed up with gunfire. "A Sauza would run into a Cuervo on the street," remembers a member of one of the families, "guns would be drawn and they would start fighting. Bang! Bang! Then another Sauza or Cuervo would be dead. Such a waste of brave men. But today there is peace and harmony among the families of Cuervo and Sauza. That is as it should be." It was Cupid, they say, who finally brought about an end to the bitter feud. A handsome Sauza romanced a comely Cuervo, love conquered enmity, and the fierce rivalry between the two leading tequileros came to a happy conclusion.*

Lee Anderson, San Diego *magazine*, *July, 1969*

*But Javier Sauza says it was romance—the marriage of his wife's aunt to a Cuervo—that ignited the feud in the first place. "My father was shot in the arm in Mexico City by Carlos Cuervo who today is a good friend of mine. As time went on no one remembered the original quarrel. They went on feuding about things they didn't even remember."*

# Tequila Ghost

2 parts tequila
1 part Pernod
½ part fresh lemon juice
Cracked ice

Shake all ingredients well with ice. Strain into cocktail glass. (1 serving)

*(From Montezuma Tequila, Barton Brands Ltd.)*

# Tequila Manhattan

2 parts gold tequila
1 part sweet vermouth
Squeeze of lime
Cherry
Orange slice

Combine the tequila, vermouth, and lime and serve on the rocks in an old-fashioned glass. Garnish with the cherry and orange slice. (1 serving)

*(From Montezuma Tequila, Barton Brands Ltd.)*

# Mexico Martini

2 ounces tequila
1 ounce dry vermouth
2 drops vanilla extract
Ice

Shake all of the ingredients with ice and strain into a chilled cocktail glass. (1 serving)

*(Montezuma Tequila, Barton Brands Ltd.)*

# The Palace Guard

Fourteen years ago a minor miracle occurred in the land of tequila when about thirty-five independent tequileros were able to set aside differences and form a joint body called the Camara Regional de la Industria Tequilera. Recent Camara president Guillermo Castaneda de Pena of Tequila San Matias, says that the purpose of this gathering of all of the agave growers and tequila producers was to maintain and protect the essence of the spirit, in production and quality, and to jointly fight the battles against ersatz tequila produced by impostors throughout the world.

That the group has continued to meet for fourteen years is, alone, a miracle acknowledged by all. So certain of the importance and permanence of the group were tequileros Beckmann, Castaneda, Nunez, Orendain, and Sauza that they pooled their pesos and purchased for the Camara a beautiful new building in Guadalajara. The membership is fully represented in the large semicircular throne with a brass footrail. Sharing the pedestal on the backbar are all of the bottles of the spirit tequila produced by the members. You guessed it—the bar dispenses only one kind of drink. Each year one of the members of this grand council is elected to serve as president.

# Tequila Pup

1 ½ ounces tequila
1 teaspoon honey
Juice of 1 lime
Dash of bitters

Shake all ingredients together. Serve in a cocktail glass. (1 serving)

*(From Montezuma Tequila, Barton Brands Ltd.)*

# Ambassador

2 ounces white tequila
2 ounces tart orange juice*
Optional: 1 ounce white sugar syrup
½ cup cracked ice

Thoroughly mix all ingredients in a blender and serve in a stemmed glass. (1 serving)

*In Mexico, the delicious juice of the naranja agria, a sour orange indigenous to Mexico, is used. It is not generally available in the United States.

*(From Tequila Sauza, Mexico)*

# Carolina

3 ounces Centenario (aged tequila)
1 ounce cream
⅓ ounce grenadine
5 drops vanilla
1 white of egg
Ground cinnamon
Maraschino cherry

Mix all ingredients, through egg white, in a blender and pour into a champagne glass. Sprinkle with a few grains of cinnamon and garnish with the cherry. (1 serving)

*(From Tequila Cuervo, Mexico)*

# The Tequila Boom

Wall Street, boards of directors, company presidents, take note. Juan Beckmann Vidal, the young operating head of Cuervo (the oldest brand in the United States, distributed since 1942, originally by Vern Underwood and now by Heublein) gives this formula for tequila's conquest. "I think we succeed with Heublein in the United States for two reasons. First, we are friends. We put more of our heart and human relations as well as money in our business with them. We opened our homes to each other.

"The second thing that makes the success is all the knowledge and all the effort and all the people that are very capable. I have great admiration for them, all the people there had faith in tequila."

# Mexican Flag Cocktail

7 ounces sugar
Juice of 5 limes
1 pint tequila
Cracked ice
4 ounces green grapes
1 jicama (scoop into balls)
4 ounces cherries

Mix the sugar with the lime juice and tequila; add a little cracked ice and mix thoroughly. Serve in cocktail glasses with a glass straw and add to each 1 grape, 1 small ball of jicama, and 1 cherry to represent the colors of the Mexican flag. (8 to 12 servings)

*Author's note:* Since the jicama is seldom available in the United States, you may only be able to represent two colors of the Mexican flag.

(*From* Mexican Cook Book *by Josefina Velazquez de Leon*)

# Cuervo Cocktail

1 ½ ounces Jose Cuervo white tequila
3 ounces pineapple juice
Sugar to taste
1 ounce lime juice
Crushed ice

Shake all ingredients well with crushed ice and serve in a champagne glass. (1 serving)

Variation: For a refreshingly different cooler, serve on the rocks with club soda.

*(From Jose Cuervo Tequila, Heublein, Inc.)*

# Tequila Cocktail

1 jigger tequila
Juice of 1 lime, strained
½ ounce grenadine or to taste
Crushed ice

Mix all of the ingredients and pour over the ice in a saucer-shaped champagne glass. Serve with a short straw. (1 serving)

*(From* The Complete Book of Mexican Cooking, *by Elisabeth Lambert Ortiz)*

# Conchita

½ ounce tequila
½ ounce grapefruit juice or soda
2-3 drops lemon juice
Ice

Mix ingredients and serve over ice. (1 serving)

*(From* San Diego *Magazine, July, 1969)*

# Tequila Daiquiri

1 ½ ounces white tequila
Juice of ½ lime
1 teaspoon powdered sugar
Ice

Vigorously shake tequila, lime, and sugar with ice and strain into a stemmed glass. (1 serving)

*(From Tequila Sauza, National Distillers Products Co.)*

# Blue Shark

1 ounce white tequila
1 ounce vodka
Dash of blue vegetable coloring

Mix all ingredients in cocktail shaker with shaved ice. Strain into cocktail glass. (1 serving)

(*From Society des Bains de Mer, Monte Carlo*)

# Cuervo Rojo (Red Crow)

1 ounce white tequila
2 ounces sangrita*
½ ounce lemon juice
Salt

Mix all ingredients but a few drops of lemon juice and the salt in a blender. Moisten the rim of a cocktail glass with the leftover lemon and then dip into the salt. Fill glass with the blended mixture. (1 serving)

*See index.

(*From Tequila Cuervo, Mexico*)

# Tequila Tasting

There is a specific vocabulary for describing the taste of wine, but how do you describe the taste of tequila? We consulted experts on both sides of the border. Their descriptions were a nonhelpful unanimous: "You *can't* describe the taste of *tequila.*"

But we knew where to go for help.

Joe Haefelin of American Distilling, a noted wine connoisseur and lecturer, is also an expert and longtime aficionado of tequila. A kindred spirit, our friend was happy to describe the divine assault of tequila upon one's senses, although even he admitted defeat in really pinpointing the essence of tequila.

"Its 'nose,' " he said, "is usually a combination of a fruity note, having some of the characteristics of pineapple with freshly grated black pepper." Beyond this, perhaps tequila simply defies description. "You just know it when you taste it," Haefelin admitted, falling prey to tequila's mystery.

Tequila's 'mouth' is unique, our connoisseur ventured. "There is really nothing in the world that resembles tequila. I think it gets back to the maguey itself. It gets back to the basic flavor of the mezcal plant after it has been cooked."

One tequila aficionado compared his preference to the versatile vodka: "Mix vodka with apple juice and you get alcoholic apple juice. Mix tequila with apple juice and you get Blossom Time."

Maybe tequila's flavor can be accurately described by the name of the next recipe.

# Earthquake

¾ ounce strawberries
1 teaspoon grenadine
1½ ounces tequila
Dash of orange bitters
Ice
Lime slice
1 fresh strawberry

In a blender combine the strawberries and grenadine. Add the tequila, bitters, and ice. Serve in a cocktail glass. Garnish with lime slice and fresh strawberry. (1 serving)

*(From Montezuma Tequila, Barton Brands Ltd.)*

# Daisy

4 ounces tequila
1 ounce lemon juice
1 ounce grenadine
1 ounce club soda
Cracked ice

Shake all ingredients well with the ice and strain into two chilled cocktail glasses. (2 servings)

*(From Jose Cuervo Tequila, Heublein, Inc.)*

# Dalia

1 jigger tequila
½ jigger triple sec or Cointreau
Juice of ½ lime
Shaved ice
Salt

Shake tequila, triple sec, and all but a few drops of lime juice well with the ice. Rub rim of glass with the remaining lime juice and dip into salt. Fill glass with the drink mixture. (1 serving)

*(From Tequila Eucario Gonzalez, Mexico)*

# Tequila Fizz

1½ ounces tequila
¾ ounce grenadine
3 ounces ginger ale
1 egg white
Crushed ice

Mix ingredients briefly in blender with a little crushed ice. Serve in small, stemmed glass. (1 serving)

*(From San Diego Magazine, July, 1969)*

# Frostbite

1 ounce tequila
½ ounce blue Curacao
½ ounce creme de cacao
2 ounces cream (or half-and-half)
Chipped ice

Pour all ingredients into blender and blend with the ice. Serve in a large cocktail or small fruit-juice glass. (1 serving) Put more win into winter and double the recipe to warm up two cool people.

(*From Pancho Villa Tequila, E. Martinoni Co.*)

# Tequila Fresa (Strawberry)

1 ½ ounces tequila
¾ ounce strawberry liqueur*
½ ounce lime juice
¼ teaspoon orange bitters
Ice
1 slice lime
1 fresh strawberry

Shake tequila, strawberry liqueur, lime juice, and bitters well with ice and strain over more ice. Garnish with fresh lime and strawberry. (1 serving)

(*From Jose Cuervo Tequila, Heublein, Inc.*)

*If strawberry liqueur is not available, use ½ cup fresh strawberries, well sugared.

# Gentle Bull

1 ½ ounces tequila
¾ ounce coffee liqueur
½ ounce heavy cream
Cracked ice

Shake all ingredients and strain into a cocktail glass. (1 serving)

(*From El Toro Tequila, The American Distilling Co.*)

# Holiday

1 ½ ounces tequila
½ ounce lemon juice
½ teaspoon grenadine
1 green cherry

Mix ingredients and serve in chilled champagne glass, garnished with the green cherry. (1 serving)

(*From* San Diego *magazine, July, 1969*)

# ¿ Mi Casa? No, ¡ Su Casa !

The incongruity of a tile roof and white stucco walls on a busy street in Chicago is forgotten once inside this beautiful home of tequila and festive cooking, Su Casa, just a few blocks off Lake Michigan in the Windy City.

The restaurant's proprietor, Ike Sewell, a passionate lover of Mexican food, travel, and drink, hired renowned architects and designers to fashion an authentic setting for his Mexican artifacts. The resulting decor and ambience recreates a veritable hacienda, restoring the glories of sixteenth century Mexico and spanning the centuries since.

Some of Su Casa's fittings include hand-carved doors with the pediment from a hacienda near Toluca, Mexico; cathedral bells dated from the 1600s; tiles hand-painted and glazed by four families in Puebla; wood sculptures representing St. Peter and St. Paul, carved in 1670 for the altar of a large Mexican cathedral; and paintings of Veracruz Indian dancers by Orozco, currently Mexico's leading artist.

Some celebrities, Chicagoans and otherwise, who frequent Ike Sewell's showplace include Chicago Black Hawks and Chicago Stadium owners Arthur and Virginia Wirtz; John and Bonnie Swearingen; the Bing Crosbys; Chicago Mayor and Mrs. Daley; Frank Sinatra; Joe Namath; and Chicago Bears owner George Halas.

Su Casa claims to be the largest tequila pouring spot in the world. Actual figures from national wholesalers substantiate the cheerful boast. Su Casa can serve 660 pilgrims per day, whereas in Mexico, places are smaller.

Popular potions at Su Casa include Margaritas, Tequila Sours, Mexitinis, Wetbacks, Tequila Cocktails, Daniel de Oros, Bandileras, Sunsets, Bloody Bulls, and Tequila Neats. Such spirited imbibing whets the appetite and paves the way for Su Casa's famous chiles rellenos, carne asada, chalupas, camarones a la Veracruzana, and tacos. The menu's chili con carne is dutifully identified as Texan (you will never find it in Mexico), and is as good a potage as you'll find anywhere — just ask celebrity Julia Meade, who always takes three or four quarts back to New York with her. For recipes, the hacienda's creator consulted the Gran Dama of Latin American cuisine, Señora Maria Luisa Lopez Figueroa de Gray (affectionately known to thousands as Bitcha, and her chosen chefs and caterers, Señora Virginia Solis and daughter, Señora Carmen Desentis.

## Daniel de Oro

1 ounce tequila
Ice
Orange juice
Creme Damiana

Pour the tequila over ice in a glass. Fill with orange juice and top with Creme Damiana. (1 serving)

*(From Su Casa Restaurant, Chicago)*

## Mexitini

1 part tequila
2 parts vermouth
1 whole chile verde (small Mexican green chile) about 1½ inches long

Combine tequila and vermouth in usual martini procedure. Garnish with the chile. (1 serving)

*(From Su Casa Restaurant, Chicago)*

## Loma Bonita (Beautiful Hill)

1 jigger tequila
2 jiggers pineapple juice
Shaved ice
Maraschino cherry

Shake ingredients well with shaved ice. Add cherry. (1 serving)

*(From Tequila Eucario Gonzalez, Mexico)*

# Icebreaker

2 ounces grapefruit juice
2 ounces white tequila
¾ ounce grenadine
½ ounce Cointreau
½ cup cracked ice

Put all ingredients into blender and mix well. Serve in a stemmed glass. (1 serving)

*(From Tequila Sauza, Mexico)*

# Latin Lover

3 dashes grenadine
½ ounce lemon juice
1 ounce tequila
1½ ounce Valentino liqueur
Cracked ice

Shake ingredients together with the ice. Strain into cocktail glass. (1 serving)

*(From El Toro Tequila, The American Distilling Co.)*

# Lolita

1½ ounces tequila
1 teaspoon honey
Juice of 1 lime
Dash of bitters
Ice

Vigorously combine all ingredients in a cocktail shaker with the ice. Pour into cocktail glass. (1 serving)

*(From Jose Cuervo Tequila, Heublein, Inc.)*

## The Great Margarita Controversy

The origin of the Margarita is, at best, controversial. Among those claiming the patent is Daniel Negrete, a seventy-five-year-old former Los Angeles bartender. Danny says an official government paper authenticating his invention of the drink exists in Mexico City. The story of his invention of the Margarita goes like this:

In 1936 Danny was the manager of the well-known Garci Crespo Hotel in Puebla, Mexico. He had a girl friend named Margarita, very beautiful, of course, who habitually took a dab of salt with whatever she had to drink. Danny decided that he would create a drink for her so she could enjoy it without having to reach into the common table salt-bowl; he would put the salt on the rim of her glass.

He chose tequila—probably that was Margarita's favorite drink. Then he decided to add Cointreau and limon juice and shake it up with ice.

The Tail of the Cock, in Los Angeles, also stakes a title to the Margarita's origin. A gringo bartender said he concocted the drink in the early fifties, and Vern Underwood, the acknowledged, aforementioned pioneer father of the contemporary tequila revival in the United States, definitely names the Tail of the Cock as the spot for the first emergence of the lady.

Around 1955 Vern sensed unusual activity in the large orders of tequila from this single restaurant and, confronting the owners, learned of the starlet who was packing patrons in to partake of the new libation. Why she was called "Margarita" is a mystery still today. But to Vern Underwood, from that day on, Margarita was to become more than a girl's name, and he said so in full-page advertisements in big circulation magazines with a picture of himself in white tie and tails with red shoes, saluting a portrait of the goddess with her cup, to "Margarita, more than a girl's name."

Mr. Acapulco, Teddy Stauffer, provides yet another source. He attributes the concoction to Margarita Sames, of San

Antonio, Texas. "Popular, vivacious Margarita Sames has been coming to Acapulco with her rancher husband for over twenty-five years," he says. "They had a house near the Flamingo Hotel and gave lots of parties. She loves tequila and drinks it all day long. She would go into a bar and ask them to mix her some tequila with Cointreau and limon and serve it in a cocktail glass. I know Margarita very well and that has always been her drink. She claims she was the first to make it a drink."

Mexican lore expert Sara Morales stakes the origin of the Margarita circa 1930 by doña Bertha, owner and bartender of Bertita's Bar in Taxco, Mexico. Bertha already had a namesake tequila drink "Bertha," therefore, the next tequila inspiration she simply called Margarita. Bertha's touch always included salt on the glass.

Last, but not least, the Caliente Race Track in Tijuana lays claim to the Margarita, surfacing there around 1930.

By now the Margarita has become such a universal symbol of tequila and Mexico that Tequilero Jaime Ruiz Llaguno says, "I think Mexico's greeting to all of its visitors should be beautiful girls dressed in Mexican costumes in the airports greeting the arrivals or bidding 'hasta la vista' to the departures with a tequila Margarita." Great idea!

Origins aside, the important matter is stirring up a good Margarita, and unless you've had one in Mexico, you haven't really had a Margarita. Here's the way they do it. Take a chilled, stemmed cocktail glass and deftly brush the rim with dry salt. The thin jacket of frost on the glass should hold the salt.

Next, scoop chipped ice into a metal shaker, add at least the necessary 1½ ounces of tequila, ½ ounce of triple sec, and 1 ounce of freshly squeezed limon juice.

Now take the final step—a gentle shaking to blend the mixture. No whirling electric gadgets to blend it and bruise it. Just a gentle, polite shaking.

Limons make the difference between a true Mexican

Margarita and all others sporting the name. A limon is a Mexican fruit with the best attributes of its parents — a lemon and a lime — and none of the bad points. The limon is tangier and tastier.

## American Legion Margarita

It's the American Legion clubhouse in Las Fuentes [Mexico], of all places, that features that most Mexican of all drinks, the Margarita. Why this is can only be guessed — the clubhouse may not be for fancypants drinkers with their complicated concoctions or it could be the Legionnaires have come all the way to Mexico to drink good Margaritas.

At any rate for ten pesos Jesus Ruiz, the bartender, puts together 1 cup of tequila, 1 cup of "Controy" orange drink and ½ cup of limon* as if he were hoisting the red, green and white of the Republic. The result is six delicious servings. Needless to say, you sit at attention and after an icy sip, salute.

(*Colony Reporter*, Guadalajara, Mexico)

*Use lime or lemon in the United States.

## Margarita in Beer Mug

4 ounces white tequila
1½ ounces triple sec
3 ounces fresh limon juice (or lime or lemon)
Ice

Put ingredients into a thoroughly chilled, 12-ounce beer mug and fill with ice. Stir and serve. (1 serving)

(*From Rafael's La Fonda del Sol, Acapulco, Mexico*)

# Sporting Life

As sporty as it is spirited, tequila follows the crowd, be it to the game or to watch. (Any modern young spectator turns into a participator when the taste sensation of the decade is passed around.)

According to Glen Campbell, tournament golfers drink their tequila straight, and for the past six years Tequila Sauza has kept them supplied at the Glen Campbell Los Angeles Open Golf Tournament, sponsored by the Junior Chamber of Commerce. What's extra nice about following this tournament is that they keep the spectators in the spirit, too, supplied with Margaritas dispensed from special little carts plying the fairways.

The Sauza tequileros get into the act on the tennis court as well, honoring stars at a recent Tucson tournament with an all-day Mexican fiesta.

# Tequini

3 ounces tequila
1 ounce dry vermouth
Ice
Twist of lemon

Stir tequila and vermouth into bar glass with ice cubes. Serve in cocktail glass garnished with lemon twist. (1 serving)

(*From* Beverage Media)

# Martini Mojado
# (Wet Martini)

Says Taco, "The Martini Mojado . . . the only difference is that it makes you laugh like mad, and that isn't all bad."

Recipe: Prepare exactly the way you make your favorite dry martini, *except use tequila instead of gin.*

*(From Eustaquio de Escandon, Mexico City and Acapulco)*


# Matador

1 ounce tequila
2 ounces pineapple juice
1 ounce lime juice
Crushed ice

Shake ingredients with ice. Serve in champagne glass or over the rocks in an old-fashioned glass. (1 serving)

Variation: Substitute tomato juice for the pineapple juice and follow the same directions. Call it a Bloody Matador.

*(From* Beverage Media)

# Mockingbird

1 ½ ounces tequila
¾ ounce crème de menthe
Crushed ice
1 ounce lime juice

Shake ingredients well with ice. Serve in chilled champagne glass. Garnish with slice of lime. Hear the birdie? (1 serving)

(*From* San Diego *Magazine, July, 1969*)

# Piñata

1 ½ ounces tequila
1 ounce banana liqueur
1 ounce lime juice
Ice

Blend ingredients with a little crushed ice until smoothly mixed. Strain into chilled, double-martini glass. (1 serving)

(*From* San Diego *Magazine, July, 1969*)

## The Marriage Cup of Popo and Ixta

The tragic love of the brave warrior Popocatepetl and the beautiful princess Ixtaccihuatl is forever enshrined in the world's most celebrated pair of snowcapped volcanoes. Mexicans continue to consummate the great love of Popo and Ixta in a marriage of their national spirit *tequila* with their exotic liqueur of the coffee bean. This "love potion" is divulged below.

One legend has it that the warrior Popocatepetl fell in love with the princess but could not have her because she was betrothed to the king. The pair eloped, and when they were discovered, fled the city, pursued by the king's troops. During their flight Princess Ixta was mortally wounded by an arrow in her back. Popo gathered her in his arms and escaped into the forest. There he gently laid her on a stone and asked the gods not let him suffer anymore. The gods, having pity on him, transformed both of the lovers into volcanoes. Today the first view of Mexico as one's plane approaches are these symbols of love: the mountaintop profile of the reclining sleeping lady—her head, breast, torso, legs, and feet, 17,454 feet high—watched over by the towering white helmet of her warrior lover 418 feet higher.

Another version has it that Ixtaccihuatl and Popocatepetl were madly in love, but the emperor offered her in marriage to any chieftain who would bring him victory in an impending battle. The fighting in progress, a rival suitor leaked word that Popo had been killed, whereupon Ixta sickened and died. In desolation, Popo had two pyramidal mountains built side by side, buried his beloved in the smaller one, and reserved the other for himself so he could keep eternal watch over her. In time both mountains grew to the immense size they are today.

Yet another version says that when Popo returned from battle and found Ixta laid to rest on top of a mountain, he was so grief-stricken that he knelt on a nearby peak to watch over her, awaiting death to join them.

# Popo e Ixta

This after-dinner drink, named for the two volcanoes, discussed in the introduction, that overlook Mexico City is usually made in one of two ways: A liqueur glass is filled ¾ full with Kahlua; then add tequila to fill glass almost to the brim. Or fill the glass with equal quantities of Kahlua and tequila. (Either way, 1 serving)

(*From* The Complete Book of Mexican Cooking, *by Elisabeth Lambert Ortiz*)

# Nupcial (Wedding)

Shaved ice
1 ounce white tequila
1⅓ ounces evaporated milk
⅔ ounce creme de cacao (white)
⅔ ounce white syrup
Maraschino cherry

Put ½ cup of shaved ice in blender and blend all ingredients for 1½ minutes. Pour into cocktail glass and garnish with a red cherry. (1 serving)

(*From Tequila Sauza, Mexico*)

# Sauzaliky

Shaved ice
4 ounces white tequila
8 ounces orange juice
½ ounce lemon juice
2 ripe bananas (medium)

Fill blender ¾ full of ice. Add all ingredients. Mix well and serve in stemmed glasses. (4 servings)

*(From Tequila Sauza, National Distillers Products Co.)*

# Tequila Sour

1½ ounces tequila
½ ounce lemon juice
1 teaspoon sugar
Ice
½ slice lemon or orange
Maraschino cherry

Shake tequila, lemon juice, and sugar well with ice. Strain into chilled whiskey-sour glass. Garnish with lemon or orange slice and cherry. (1 serving)

*(From Jose Cuervo Tequila, Heublein, Inc.)*

# Sourteq

1 ½ ounces tequila
1 ounce lemon juice
1 teaspoon sugar
2 dashes aromatic bitters
Ice
Maraschino cherry
Fresh orange or lemon slice

Shake tequila, juice, sugar, and bitters in bar glass with ice. Strain into sour glass prepared with cherry and slice of orange or lemon. (1 serving)

Variation: Pour the drink over ice cubes in highball glass; fill with soda water and stir. This turns a Sourteq into a Tall Sour.

(*From* Beverage Media)

# Stinger

1 ½ ounces gold tequila
¾ ounce white crème de menthe
Ice

Shake ingredients with cracked ice and strain into cocktail glass. If preferred, ingredients may be poured over fine ice in cocktail glass. Serve with short straw. (1 serving)

(*From Tequila Sauza, National Distillers Products Co.*)

# Strawberry Rita

Sugar
2 ounces fresh strawberries plus 1 or 2 sliced strawberries (for
    garnish)
1 ounce tequila
1 ounce plain bar syrup
Ice
Lime slice
Whipped cream (optional)

Sugar the rim of a deep wine glass. In a blender mix the
strawberries, tequila, syrup, and some ice. Pour into the glass
and garnish with the lime slice, sliced strawberries, and
whipped cream. (1 serving)

(*From* Texas Monthly, *September, 1975*)

# Sunset

1½ ounces tequila
½ ounce lime juice
½ ounce grenadine
Ice
1 slice lime

Put tequila, lime juice, grenadine, and ½ cup crushed ice into
blender. Blend at low speed 10–15 seconds. Pour into chilled
old-fashioned glass. Garnish with lime slice. Fill glass with ice.
(1 serving)

(*From Jose Cuervo Tequila, Heublein, Inc.*)

# Tequila a la Canela
# (Tequila with Cinnamon)

Into an old fashion glass put:

1 ounce Cuervo Almendrado (tequila liqueur available in Mexico)
1½ ounces condensed milk
Ground cinnamon

Stir liqueur and condensed milk in an old-fashioned glass, adding with a small spoon ground cinnamon to taste. (1 serving)

*(From Tequila Cuervo, Mexico)*

# Toreador

1½ ounces tequila
½ ounce creme de cacao
Ice
Whipped cream
Powdered cocoa

Shake tequila and creme de cacao with crushed ice, strain into cocktail glass and top sparingly with whipped cream. Sprinkle lightly with cocoa. (1 serving)

*(From Jose Cuervo Tequila, Heublein, Inc.)*

# 4

# Cups, Punches,
# and Other Mixtures

## ¡A Su Salud!

Remembering that tequila is a mezcal, a maxim for the proverbial medicine chest: *Para todo mal mezcal, y para todo bien tambien.* (As a remedy for everything bad, mezcal . . . and to celebrate all good as well.)

Many amigos will raise tequila-filled glasses in toast to each other's health, and they think gringos should follow suit. Natural love of the stuff is not the only reason to drink tequila. It also, according to many Mexicans, purifies the blood, cures dysentery, and calms the nursing baby, says Lee Anderson in *San Diego* magazine. Also, tequila is popular as an after-shave lotion, for disinfecting cuts, and has a remarkable reputation as an aphrodisiac.

Tequila as elixir certainly is not unreasonable. The cooked heart of its plant source, the agave, has yielded a highly nutritious food, mexcalli, since the time of the Aztec civilization. Ancient hieroglyphics show Aztecs cooking the mexcalli in ovens dug in the ground.

The cooking process converts the agave's starch into glucose and dextrose, or, in other words, carbohydrates. It was in cooking the agave for food that these ancient peoples discovered that, when left to macerate in water, fermentation took place — producing a good wine.

The first technical essay on the cultivation of the maguey, or agave, and on the manufacture of tequila, published in 1887, included this summary of the therapeutic and hygienic qualities of the drink-cum-elixir, then most often called mezcal wine:

The virtues of this drink, confirmed by experience, are: to awaken the natural appetite for food in persons who, for some reason, have lost it; to aid in digestion; to invigorate the gastric functions; to have a real effect in those illnesses in which anatomy plays a leading role, and in dyspepsias that resist all known agents of therapeutics; to cause superficial wounds to heal rapidly, and with a single application, when they are washed and treated with it; to ease pain and prevent, generally, the inflammation consequent to sprains, applying it in fomentations; to invigorate organic functions, weakened by age; to slake the thirst occasioned by sunstroke, a property utilized with great success by many travelers, thus preventing the illnesses, sometimes fatal, resulting when, to satisfy that imperious necessity, they drink water; to moderate notably the effects upon the organism produced, on certain occasions, by an unusual drop in temperature; to calm the unpleasant sensation of hunger for a period of several hours, because it is one of the so-called respiratory foods; to revive the strength drained by excessive work, stimulate the intelligence, banish boredom, and produce pleasant illusions. But understand well: only by using this liquor in due moderation and at the proper time will the healthful, hygienic or moral affects just mentioned be produced. Otherwise, it will only produce drunkenness, with all the physical and immoral consequences that chronic or acute alcoholism brings with it, and which are of the most lamentable significance to the individual, the family, and society.

*Study on Maguey*
Lazaro Perez

Around the same time, The London Medical Society gave a nod in the direction of tequila's medicinal qualities and welcomed its appearance on European markets as a significant contribution of North America to the rest of the world.

# Hairy Dog

This is a prescription for the blahs, the blues, the "brown whimpers," the general malaise that can overtake even the sturdy and temperate person.

Ice
6 ounces canned Clamato juice
   or 3 ounces clam juice and
   3 ounces tomato juice
1 ½ ounces tequila
½ teaspoon hot prepared horseradish

Pour the juice, or juices, over the ice. Add the tequila and horseradish and stir well. Sip slowly until circulation is restored. (1 serving)

*(From Pancho Villa Tequila, E. Martinoni Co.)*

# Throat Coater

For the aches and miseries of the uncommon cold: In a large mug or hot drink glass mix 4 ounces (yes, 4 ounces) of lemon juice with 3 tablespoons of honey and 2 ounces of tequila. Fill to the brim with very hot water and stir. Drink this potion in a quiet, darkened room preceded by two aspirin and followed by a nap.

*(From Pancho Villa Tequila, E. Martinoni Co.)*

# The Godhead of Tequila

In the land of tequila, the ancient gods of the agave have been re-enshrined. The god of Mezcal, Mextli, who also gave his name to Mexico, rules the fertility of the earth. The female personification of the agave is Mayahuel, who, with her 400 nursing breasts, also presides over fertility.

# Christmas Punch

1 pound loaf sugar
3 lemons
2 oranges
1 quart hot, black and green teas, mixed
1 quart aged dark rum
1 quart good sherry
½ bottle aged tequila
2 quarts 7-Up

Place the sugar in a punch bowl; grate upon it the rinds of 3 lemons and the juice of 2. Add the juice of 2 oranges. Pour over the hot tea. Stir well and put aside to cool, covering tightly to prevent any escape of the aroma.

When the mixture has cooled, add the rum, sherry, and tequila. Mix well. Set the punch bowl in a snow of ice until it is well chilled and ready for use; then add the 7-Up. (44 4-oz. servings)

*(From Tequila San Matias, Mexico)*

## Aztec Punch

1 gallon tequila
Juice of 12 lemons
4 16-ounce cans grapefruit juice
2 quarts strong tea
1 ½ teaspoons cinnamon
1 ½ ounces bitters

Pour all of the ingredients into a large punch bowl. Chill in the refrigerator for at least 2 hours. Stir well before serving. (124 cups)

*(From Montezuma Tequila, Barton Brands Ltd.)*

## Nice 'N Easy Punch Bowl

Ice
1 13 ¼ -ounce can pineapple chunks, undrained
1 bottle tequila (a fifth)
2 large bottles lemon-lime soda, chilled

Place block of ice or 2 trays of ice cubes and pineapple chunks, with juice, in a large punch bowl. Pour tequila over. Stir. Add soda and stir again — just once. Serve immediately in small punch cups, with a pineapple chunk in each portion. (About 25 servings)

*(From Ole Tequila, Schenley Imports Co.)*

# T-Bone (or Teabone)

Brewed or instant tea (hot)
1½ ounces tequila
lemon

Prepare a tea of your choice. Add tequila. Squeeze a few drops of lemon. Serve with a lemon wedge and drink it hot. (1 serving)

Variation: Try spicing it up with cloves or cinnamon.

*(From Montezuma Tequila, Barton Brands Ltd.)*

# Tropicana

1 whole pineapple
Ice (cubes and shaved)
Juice of ½ lime
1 ounce tequila
1 ounce framboise
Dash of grenadine

Cut the top from a fresh pineapple, leaving its leaves intact, and scoop out the meat. Leave a wall at least ¾ inch thick. Chill the shell and the top in the refrigerator. Force the scooped-out fruit through a food mill or whirl it in an electric blender to press out the juice, and strain it.

In a cocktail shaker with ice cubes, combine 2 ounces of the pineapple juice with the lime juice, tequila, framboise, and grenadine. Shake briskly.

Fill the chilled pineapple shell ⅓ full with shaved ice. Strain in the drink and cover with the pineapple top. Serve with a straw. (1 serving)

*(From Tequila San Matias, Mexico)*

## Tequila-Pineapple Liqueur

Fill a 1-quart jar halfway with chunks of ripe pineapple. Pour tequila to the brim. Add 1 teaspoon sugar (optional). Cap jar and place in refrigerator for 24 hours. Drain off liquid and serve as an after-dinner liqueur. (Approx. 16 1-oz. servings)

*(From Montezuma Tequila, Barton Brands Ltd.)*

# Mogul

1 teaspoon instant coffee
2 teaspoons instant cocoa mix
Boiling water
1½ ounces tequila
Whipped cream

Combine the instant coffee and the cocoa mix in a mug with boiling water. Pour in the tequila and top with a dab of whipped cream. (1 serving)

*(From Montezuma Tequila, Barton Brands Ltd.)*

## Sunrise Punch

4 quarts orange drink
1 quart fruit punch
1 quart tequila
8 ounces grenadine
Fresh lemon and orange slices (for garnish)

Mix all ingredients, garnish with lemon and orange slices, and serve over ice. (30 servings)

*(From Canfield Bottlers and Pancho Villa Tequila, E. Martinoni Co.)*

# The Real Coco Loco

The origin of the coco loco is claimed by Acapulco, where palm trees are everywhere, laden the year round (since "cocos", as they are called there, have no specific maturation season) with fresh coconuts. In the Guerrero countryside, along the road or in the fields, campesinos wanting a cool fresh drink spot the nearest palm tree, shinny up the tree with ever-present machete, fell a fat green coco, chop a 2 or 3-inch hole in the top, and quaff the natural zesty water. Hence, with the addition of some aguardiente. . . . the crazy coconut.

On the road from Acapulco south to San Marcos, sidling the Laguna de Tres Palos, "Las Palmiras" also dispenses the coco loco in its native habitat. There Petra and her father maintain a palapa strung with hammocks where the lake breezes rock the siesta-seeking locals. Miguel took me (Marion, the coauthor) there many times on horseback where Petra, in her lean-to kitchen taught me to make tortillas by hand, sopes, and caldo de camarones (lake shrimp in broth), and, of course, the local tequila specialty. The five towering palm trees that shade the palapa also supply the primary component for the real coco loco—the fresh coconut in its green shell. Here is Petra's formula. The author offers testimony that ensconced in an hamaca, it's very easy to drink one. . . . two. . .

## Coco Loco De Petra

1 ounce tequila
1 ounce gin
1 ounce rum
Coconut water (in the fresh coconut or canned)
½ ounce grenadine
Squeeze of limon (lemon or lime in U.S.)

Mix all ingredients together in a very fresh coconut or in a very tall highball glass. Add ice, a straw, and drink.

## Cities of Drink

"Guadalajara, Mexico City, and Acapulco are Mexico's drinking centers," bar chief Jorge Zarate says. "Because of its altitude, Mexico City relies on international drinks like Manhattans and Martinis. But in Acapulco and Guadalajara you'll find the warm-weather drinks, and tequila gives Guadalajara special distinction in this department. This city's defenders against spring heat are not its fountains, trees, or buildings, but its bartenders—tireless soldiers indeed. As the day warms, the rows of drinkers deepen until the 'cantinero,' measuring and mixing, stirring and shaking, swelters in the juices of his sacrifice."

# Coco Loco

½ ounce tequila
½ ounce rum
½ ounce gin
½ ounce sweet syrup
1 ounce pineapple juice
½ ounce limon (or lime or lemon)
Coconut water
Ice

Mix all ingredients in a half of a coconut shell and add coconut water and ice until brimful. (1 serving)

*(From Marriott Hotel, Guadalajara, Mexico)*

# Cuervo Punch

White tequila, any amount desired
1 quart cranberry juice
1 quart soda water
1 6-ounce can frozen lemonade

Stir all ingredients into punch bowl, over large chunk of ice. (Approx. 20 4-oz. servings)

*(From Jose Cuervo Tequila, Heublein, Inc.)*

# Holiday Punch

Prepare an extract of 1 dozen plums in 2 quarts of water. Add 1 sprig of cinnamon bark. Boil ¼ hour. Add 2 cups of tequila and add sugar to taste. Serve in cups, adding 1 cooked plum to each. (Approx. 20 4-oz. servings)

*(From Tequila Eucario Gonzalez, Mexico)*

## Bloody Bullski

3 ounces beef broth (or instant beef bouillon mix)
3 ounces tomato juice
1½ ounces tequila
Seasoning

Heat beef broth and tomato juice to boiling point. Pour into mug. Add tequila. Season to taste. (1 serving)

*(From Montezuma Tequila, Barton Brands Ltd.)*

## Summer Punch

½ pound strawberries
4 ounces sugar
2 cups water
2 cups tequila
Ice

Mix all ingredients in a blender. Add ice and serve. (Approx. 12 4-oz. servings)

*(From Tequila Eucario Gonzalez, Mexico)*

## Tio Maurice

Drink ¼ bottle of tequila. Peel an orange in one continuous strip; put orange peel and a little sugar in bottle with remaining tequila. Cap the bottle and allow to sit while you recover from drinking the first quarter of the bottle. Sip after dinner as you would any liqueur.

*(From* Texas Monthly, *September, 1975)*

Photo by M. Gorman

# 5

# Tequila Cookery

## The Mexican Stove

Richard Condon, author of the widely read *Manchurian Candidate, Mile High,* and *The Vertical Smile,* went down to Mexico several years ago to absorb some background for his novel *A Talent for Loving.* He fell in love with the country, particularly with its culinary traditions, and with his daughter Wendy Bennett wrote a beautiful exaltation to the garden of Mexico — *The Mexican Stove.* No one could say it better than they in this delightful excerpt: "Mexicans tend to be healthy, humorous, and full of bounce; their food has similar qualities. To cook and eat Mexican food is to celebrate sensuality. It is an aphrodisiac that excites one's passion for living. . . ."

What secret lies behind this gourmet excitement? It could just be a dash of tequila.

## Traditional Tequila Tasties

In tequila country, certain appetizers or hors d'oeuvres — one might call them enhancements — are served as accompaniments to the drinking of tequila. Among them are queso (cheese) cut into bite-sized chunks; small pig knuckles in vinaigrette; braised pork bits called carnitas; and two delicious snacks "reciped" or described here — pico de gallo and Charales.

# Pico de Gallo

Literally translated, *pico de gallo* means "beak of the rooster," but its culinary translation is something else altogether. The French have something similar called *crudites*—mixed raw vegetables and fruits—but the south-of-the-border version somehow seems a little more toothsome. In many bars and restaurants in Mexico the only way to miss a pico de gallo when you order tequila is to ask the waiter *not* to bring it.

To assemble your own pico—the refreshing, nonfattening way to munch—make a platter of wedged-shaped (beak-shaped) cuts of:

1 orange
1 cucumber
1 pineapple
1 jicama (seldom available in the United States)

Cut the orange into ⅜-inch slices. Cut each slice into quarters. Peel the cucumber and cut it into ⅜-inch slices. If large in diameter, cut slices in half. Peel and slice the pineapple. Cut slices into wedges. Section the jicama (if unavailable, no substitution is necessary—the first three items will do). Sprinkle the arrangement with a little red chili powder—or paprika, for a somewhat decreased bite).

# Charales

Charales are tiny fishes, about 2 inches in length head to tail. They are deep-fried and eaten with the fingers, like chips. Indigenous to Lake Chapala, east of Guadalajara, in tequila land, charales must be reserved as a special treat when visiting Guadalajara and its environs.

# Parade of Pig En Plato or:
# Mexican Dissertation on Roast Pig

A feast of roast pig in tequila country is one of the greatest of Mexican gastronomic pleasures. Every part of the pig is used to prepare tasty dishes for this traditional meal. A tequila conchita (see recipe in chapter 3) is a very refreshing warm-weather libation to be sipped with the pre-meal accompaniments of guacamole and tortillas.

The first course is "pork hands" (as pig's feet are called in Mexico), cooked and served cold with a vinaigrette. Next, consomme made with pork broth from the pig's head is served from a great tureen, followed by arroz rojo (red rice, similar to fried rice, made with tomato).

Then, the pork skin, fried but not crisp, called *cueritos,* is served cold with vinaigrette along with another variation of cooked skin called *chicharron.* Two types of chicharron are served. One type is the ¼-inch-thick outer skin, which is fried; the other is the second layer of the skin which has fat on it next to the meat. Some of the meat is left attached to the skin, and this is also fried and usually sandwiched in tacos.

The remainder of the pork is all meat (Mexican pigs are characteristically lean and delicate). The meat is cut like chops, sauteed in the pork fat, and served with rice, avocado, and fried beans. The blood of the pig is used in a dish called *rellena,* which means stuffing. It is like a sausage stuffing—the blood mixed with spices, tomatoes, chilies, onions, and rice—but it is not stuffed into a skin because it is eaten immediately, served on tacos.

Then the organ meats—heart, liver, kidneys—all are chopped very fine, cooked with spices, and served in small tortillas like soft tacos.

Finally, after all the parts of the pig have been served and consumed, the feasting is concluded with panelas (sweet rolls) and assorted Mexican candies.

*Juan Beckman Vidal*
*Tequila Cuervo, Mexico*

# Mexican Round-Up

This is the menu for the Mexican buffet served to the late Mike Roy, CBS radio personality, by Francisco Xavier Sauza in April, 1975, during Roy's visit to tequila country.

## Botanas

Quesadillas de flor de calabaza —tortillas filled with fried pumpkin flowers

Taquitos—small tortillas stuffed with chicken or beef and deep fried

Nachos—small tostadas with beans, grilled cheese, and chile jalapeno

Canapes de langosta —lobster hors d'oeuvres

Tortitas de camaron—small shrimp patties

Sopes—small hollowed out tortilla patties filled with refried beans, cheese, and lettuce

## Buffet

Huitlacoche —a special Mexican delicacy made with the fungi that grows on ears of corn

Verdolagas con espinazo—pork marrow with special Mexican purslane

Carnitas estilo Tepatitlan—steamed pork meat

Camarones al tequila —shrimps with tequila sauce

Pollo en pipian—chicken in a mild chile sauce based on ground pumpkin seeds

Frijoles de la olla —whole beans cooked in clay pot (cazuela)

Frijoles refritos con chile de arbol—refried beans with tree chile

Chiles rellenos con queso y carne—stuffed chiles with cheese and beef

Arroz a la Mexicana —Mexican rice

Guacamole

Nopales — salad of cactus
Salsa Mexicana — Mexican sauce
Tamales surtidos — variety of tamales stuffed with meat, green
or red sauce, sweet cheese, etc.
Ceviche — raw fish marinated in lime juice, onions, tomatoes,
etc.
Bunuelos — dessert
Charales — small fish fried in oil
Frijoles negros con hepazote — black beans cooked with a
Mexican herb called hepazote
Mangos flambe

# Avocado Cream

| | |
|---|---|
| 1 cup sour cream | 1-2 tablespoons tequila |
| ⅓ cup mayonnaise | ½ teaspoon onion powder |
| 1 ripe avocado | ½ teaspoon garlic powder |
| (pared and pitted) | ½ teaspoon salt |
| 2 tablespoons lemon or | Freshly ground pepper to taste |
| lime juice | |
| ¼ cup minced dill or | |
| 1 tablespoon dill weed | |

Combine sour cream, mayonnaise, avocado, and lemon juice
together in a blender. Turn blender on and off for 1-minute
intervals until ingredients are perfectly smooth. Add dill,
tequila, onion powder, garlic powder, salt, and pepper. Puree
until ingredients are mixed well. Spoon over fish, vegetables,
or salads; also delicious as a dip. (2 cups)

(By *Anna Muffoletto/Cordon Bleu of New York, Ltd. for El Toro Tequila*)

# Crab Dip

3 8-ounce packages cream cheese
3 6-ounce cans lump crab meat
2 teaspoons prepared mustard
2 teaspoons confectioners' sugar
1 teaspoon onion juice
Garlic salt, to taste
Seasoning salt, to taste
¼ cup tequila

Put all ingredients in the top of a double boiler. Stir over heat until well-blended and slightly foamy. Serve with dip-pables — crackers, toast rounds, crunchy vegetables. (About 1⅓ quarts)

*(From Jean Hepler, Stamford, Connecticut)*

# Liver Pate

About 1 pound thinly sliced bacon
¼ cup plus 1 tablespoon tequila
1 pound calf's liver
1 pound beef, pork, or lamb liver
½ pound ground veal
2 eggs, beaten
½ teaspoon finely chopped garlic
Salt
Freshly cracked white pepper
3 or 4 chicken livers
1 bunch crisp watercress

Preheat the oven to 300° F. Line a pate mold with half the bacon slices and sprinkle with 1 tablespoon tequila. Put the livers and the ground veal through a fine meat grinder twice.

Then beat the ground meats with the beaten eggs, chopped garlic, salt, and freshly cracked pepper in the mixer. Heat ¼ cup tequila in a little pan, ignite, and pour it on to the liver mixture, and beat again. Put half of the mixture in the prepared mold. Arrange the chicken livers in a row down the center. Cover them with the rest of the ground meat mixture. Cover the top of the pate with the remaining slices of bacon. Wrap the filled mold with aluminum foil and set it in a roasting pan half-filled with hot water. Bake for 1½ hours. Remove and allow the pate to cool in the mold in the water. Set a brick on top of it while it is cooling. Then set the mold in the refrigerator to chill for 24 hours.

To serve, turn the pate out of the mold and onto a serving platter. Cut a few slices and arrange them overlapping in front of the uncut piece. Garnish with watercress.

# Pepitos

Created by Carmen Lopez Figueroa and available on call in most restaurants and hotels throughout Mexico, pepitos have been described as the *best sandwiches in the world*.

*Simple salsa Mexicana*

½ cup chopped tomato pulp (a tomato skinned, seeded, and
    chopped)
¼ cup chopped onion
¼ cup fresh or canned chili verde (green, hot chili peppers)
½ teaspoon salt

*Sandwich*

8 French dinner rolls* (oval shaped, with hard crusts and soft
    centers)
1 pound skirt or flank steak (or tenderloin, if you're going
    deluxe)
3 tablespoons butter
¼ cup tequila

First prepare the simple salsa Mexicana (also called *salsa cruda*). Mix together the chopped tomato, onion, chili peppers, and salt. Set aside. Split the rolls in half, then wrap them in foil and keep them warm in a preheated oven, 400° F.

Cut the steak, on the slant, into 16 slices about ¼ inch thick (2 slices per roll). Melt the butter in a saute pan. When it is very hot and sizzling, add the slices of steak (a few at a time, making sure that they do not touch each other, or they will not brown). Brown each slice quickly on each side and set aside. When all slices are browned, return all the steak to the pan. Pour the tequila over the meat and ignite. When the flame dies down, set the steak aside.

To assemble the pepitos: Spoon a little of the pan juice on the inside of each warmed roll. Put two slices of steak on the bottom half of each roll and cover with the top half. Serve the Salsa Mexicana as an accompaniment to be spooned on top of the steak, allowing each person to use the quantity desired. (4 servings, 2 pepitos each)

*One of Mexico's legacies from its French period is the know-how for making excellent French bread and dinner rolls. So Mexico has the best breads of both worlds—tortillas and French bread.

## Welsh Rarebit

2 tablespoons sweet butter
2 egg yolks, beaten
2 whole eggs, beaten
1 cup semi-soft cheese, such as Swiss, grated
¼ cup sour cream
Salt to taste
A few grains cayenne pepper
1 teaspoon dry mustard
2 tablespoons tequila
8 toast fingers

Put all of the ingredients except the toast in the top of a double boiler and stir over low heat until the mixture achieves a smooth thick consistency. Spoon it into a warmed au gratin or shallow serving dish. Surround with the toast. (4 servings)

# Cheese Fondue

3 eggs, well beaten
½ cup cream
1 cup freshly grated Swiss cheese
1 tablespoon butter
¼ cup tequila
½ teaspoon dry mustard
Salt
A few grains cayenne pepper
8 toast fingers

Combine all of the ingredients (except the toast) in the top of a double boiler and stir over low heat until the mixture comes to a stiff consistency. Serve in a warm shallow dish accompanied with the toast fingers.

*Author's note:* Or try your own favorite cheese fondue recipe, substituting tequila for kirsch.

## Crab and Avocado Au Gratin

1 pound crab meat, coarsely flaked
1 large ripe avocado, coarsely chopped
2 medium-size ripe tomatoes, skinned, seeded, and shredded
⅔ cup dry bread crumbs
4 tablespoons butter, melted
1 cup finely chopped onion
¾ cup freshly grated Parmesan cheese
2 tablespoons capers
½ teaspoon curry powder
Salt
Freshly cracked white pepper
Cayenne pepper
½ teaspoon Worcestershire sauce
Tabasco sauce
6 tablespoons tequila (preferably añejo)
2 tablespoons vegetable oil
¾ cup sour cream
2 tablespoons chopped fresh chives

Preheat the oven to 350° F. In a mixing bowl combine the flaked crab meat, chopped avocado, shredded tomato, 2 tablespoons bread crumbs, melted butter, chopped onion, 2 tablespoons grated Parmesan cheese, and capers, and mix thoroughly. Add the curry powder, salt, freshly cracked white pepper, a few grains cayenne pepper, Worcestershire sauce, a little Tabasco sauce, and mix again. Fill 6 4-6-inch baking shells with this mixture. Drizzle 1 tablespoon tequila over each serving. Sprinkle the remaining bread crumbs and grated cheese over the top. Dot with a few drops of vegetable oil. Bake for 20-25 minutes.

In a small saucepan, mix the sour cream and the chives and season with a little salt and cayenne pepper. Warm the mixture a little and about 5 minutes before the shells are to be removed from the oven, pour a little of the warmed cream over each. (6 servings)

# Quiche Lorraine

*Pastry*

2 cups all-purpose flour
2 hard-boiled egg yolks, strained
3 egg yolks (raw)
8 tablespoons butter, cut into small pieces
½ teaspoon dry mustard
1 teaspoon salt
1 teaspoon paprika
2 tablespoons freshly grated Parmesan cheese

*Filling*

12 slices bacon, cut in shreds
3 whole eggs
2 egg yolks
¾ cup cream, scalded
¼ cup white tequila
5 tablespoons grated Parmesan cheese
Salt
Cayenne pepper
Paprika

First make the pastry. Preheat the oven to 350° F. Put the flour on a board or marble slab and make a well in the center. Into the well put the strained hard-boiled egg yolks, 3 raw egg yolks, butter, dry mustard, 1 teaspoon salt, 1 teaspoon paprika, and 2 tablespoons grated cheese. Work the center ingredients to a smooth paste. Then work in the flour, using the heel of your hand. Shape the dough into a ball, wrap it in wax paper or plastic, and let it stay in the refrigerator for 1 hour. Roll it out and line a 10-inch flan ring set on a jelly roll pan or cookie sheet. Neatly trim off the top edge. Line the dough with a piece of wax paper and anchor the paper with about ½ cup of raw rice. Bake for 30 minutes.

Now make the filling: Reduce the oven temperature to 300° F. Cook the bacon shreds until they are crisp and lightly browned. Drain them and reserve the fat. Beat the eggs and egg yolks and add the cream, tequila, 2 tablespoons grated cheese, a pinch of salt, a few grains of cayenne pepper, the bacon and the reserved bacon fat. Spoon the filling into the baked pastry and bake until it is set, about 30–45 minutes. Before serving, sprinkle the top of the quiche with the rest of the grated cheese and a few dashes of paprika. (6–8 servings)

## Chili Pepper and Onion Tart

*Tart shell*

1 cup all-purpose flour
½ teaspoon salt
½ teaspoon finely grated lemon rind
6 tablespoons butter
3 tablespoons white tequila, well chilled
A little melted butter (about 2–3 teaspoons)

*Filling*

2 tablespoons dry bread crumbs
½ cup plus 2 tablespoons freshly grated Parmesan cheese
⅓ cup plus 2 tablespoons melted butter
2 Bermuda onions, sliced ½ inch thick
3 whole eggs plus 2 egg yolks
1 teaspoon dry mustard
1 teaspoon Dijon mustard
1 teaspoon salt
¼ teaspoon cayenne pepper
2½ cups milk, scalded
¼ cup of diced green chilies
1 tablespoon white tequila
Dash chili powder or paprika

Preheat the oven to 350° F. Sift the flour with the salt into a bowl. Add the lemon rind. Cut the butter into pieces and rub it into the flour with the fingertips until the mixture resembles coarse cornmeal. Use the very cold tequila to work the dough into a firm paste. Roll the pastry out on a lightly floured surface until it is large enough to line a 10-inch-diameter flan ring or pie pan. Lay the dough over the rolling pin and transfer it to the pan, placing it loosely over the pan. With the fingers, shape it firmly into the pan and trim off the excess dough. Shape the top edge evenly and trim all around with pastry pincers. Brush the bottom of the pastry with a little melted butter. Line the pastry shell with wax paper. To keep the paper down, put rice, beans, or rock salt on the paper.

Bake the pastry shell in the preheated oven for 30 minutes. Remove the wax paper and the rice, beans, or salt. Return the shell to the oven and bake another 10–15 minutes, until it is golden brown all over. Leave the oven temperature at 350° F.

Make the filling: Place the baked tart shell on a baking sheet for support. Sprinkle the bottom of the shell with a mixture of the bread crumbs and 2 tablespoons of the Parmesan cheese. In 2 tablespoons of the melted butter, in a saucepan, cook the sliced Bermuda onions until soft. In a separate bowl mix the eggs and extra egg yolks with a whisk. Stir in the 2 mustards, the salt, and cayenne pepper. Blend well but do not beat. Allow the remaining ⅓ cup melted butter to cool and then stir it into the egg mixture. Mix in half (¼ cup) of the remaining Parmesan cheese and the scalded milk. Combine the diced green chilies with the tequila and add to the cheese mixture, along with the cooked Bermuda onions. When all ingredients are combined, spoon into the tart shell and bake for 20 minutes, or until set.

When the tart is baked, top evenly with the remaining ¼ cup Parmesan cheese. Then sprinkle the chili powder or paprika all over. Serve warm. (6–8 servings)

## Salute to Mexico Salad

Tequila is the national drink of Mexico, and here's a salad designed to salute its national colors — red, white, and green.

*Dressing*

1 teaspoon coarse salt
2 teaspoons freshly ground white pepper
¼ teaspoon sugar
1 teaspoon dry mustard
1 teaspoon Dijon mustard
1 teaspoon lemon juice
2 tablespoons tarragon vinegar
3 tablespoons olive oil
7 tablespoons vegetable oil
1 egg

*Salad*

1 head Boston lettuce
1 romaine lettuce heart
2 Belgian endives
1 thin cucumber, peeled, seeded, and cut into ½-inch cubes
½ pound young spinach leaves
About 8 scallions, cut in ½-inch lengths
4 small, ripe tomatoes, skinned and cut into ½-inch cubes
½ cup chopped fresh parsley
1 heaping tablespoon thick sour cream

First, make the dressing. Put all the ingredients in a screw-top jar and shake thoroughly. Pour the dressing into the bottom of a large round salad bowl.

Now make the salad. Break the Boston lettuce and romaine lettuce heart into bite-sized pieces and put them in the bowl on top of the dressing. Cut the endives into 1-inch pieces and scatter them on top of the lettuce. Scatter the cubed cucumber on top of the endives and arrange the spinach leaves, broken into bite-sized pieces, if you want, on top of the endives and cucumber. Pile the scallions, like a bull's eye, in the center. Arrange the cubed tomatoes in a circle around the scallions, leaving a margin of spinach showing around the edge of the dish. Sprinkle the chopped fresh parsley over the spinach border. Put a large dollop of thick sour cream on top of the scallions in the center. Cover the bowl with plastic wrap and store in the refrigerator until the salad is to be eaten. Then toss and serve.

## Sangrita Aspic Ring

3½ cups strained, fresh, tart orange juice
6 teaspoons Bufalo Salsa Picante
1 teaspoon Worcestershire sauce
2 teaspoons coarse salt
2 teaspoons grenadine
1 teaspoon fresh lemon juice
2 tablespoons tomato paste
¼ cup tequila
3 tablespoons unflavored gelatine
Bunch of crisp, fresh watercress
Wedges of lime or lemon

Combine 1 cup orange juice, Bufalo salsa picante, Worcestershire sauce, salt, grenadine, lemon juice, tomato paste, tequila, and gelatine in a saucepan and stir over low heat until the mixture comes to a boil and the gelatine is dissolved. Stir the mixture into the remaining orange juice. Set the mixture over ice cubes and stir until it begins to thicken. Pour it into a 1-quart ring mold and put it in the refrigerator to set.

When the aspic is firmly set, remove it from the mold; run a small, sharp, heated knife around the edge of the mold to ease it. Then dip the whole mold into hot water and quickly invert it onto a chilled serving platter. Garnish with clusters of watercress and lime or lemon wedges. (4 servings)

*Author's Note:* This zesty aspic may be served with toasted tortilla chips or you may wish to fill the center with cold boiled shrimps moistened with a little mayonnaise. The aspic also may be served as a madrilene, in iced soup cups, garnished with finely chopped fresh chives and a wedge of lime. The Bufalo Salsa Picante ingredient is one of the most popular sauces in Mexico and now is available in some of the Mexican food specialty stores in New York, such as Casa Moneo. If you cannot get it, you can obtain a reasonable substitute with a few drops of Tabasco and 1 additional tablespoon tomato paste.

## Tequila and Beer Soup

1 quart beer (preferably Mexican)
¼ cup granulated brown sugar
1 small stick cinnamon, or
  ¼ teaspoon powdered cinnamon
1 small ginger root
The grated rind of 1 lemon
1 whole egg
2 egg yolks
4 tablespoons all-purpose flour
½ cup milk
4 tablespoons butter
4 tablespoons tequila
½ cup heavy cream, whipped, or ¾ cup thick sour cream

Combine the beer, sugar, cinnamon, ginger root, and lemon rind in a heavy pan and simmer for 5 minutes. In another saucepan, not over heat, mix together the whole egg, egg yolks, and flour. When the mixture is absolutely smooth, stir in the milk. Melt the butter in a little pan. Off the heat add the tequila to the butter and stir this mixture into the egg mixture. Strain the hot beer into the egg mixture and stir with a wire whisk until it is smooth. Stir the soup over very low heat for 10 minutes, taking care that the soup does not boil. Just before serving quickly fold in the whipped or sour cream. (4–6 servings)

# Boula con Tequila

This is one of Dione Lucas's variations of her green pea and turtle soup, which she called Boula.

3 cups shelled fresh green peas,
   or 2 packages frozen green peas
1 medium onion, sliced
3 tablespoons butter
Salt
3 tablespoons all-purpose flour
1 large can green turtle soup
1 cup light cream
¼ cup tequila añejo
1 cup heavy cream, whipped

Cook the peas and sliced onion in 1 cup of water with the butter and salt, covered. Frozen peas will be tender in 4 or 5 minutes; fresh peas will take a little longer. By the time the peas are tender, most of the water will have evaporated. Off the heat stir in the flour. Strain the turtle soup, reserving the turtle meat, and add the broth to the pea mixture. Bring the soup to a boil over moderate heat, stirring constantly. Reduce the heat and let the soup simmer gently for 2 or 3 minutes. Then rub the soup through a fine vegetable strainer. Add the light cream, tequila, and turtle meat. Taste for seasoning. Heat the soup thoroughly.

To serve, ladle the soup into individual soup bowls, top each with a dollop of whipped cream, and brown quickly under the broiler. Serve at once. (4-6 servings)

## Sopa de Aguacate
## (Avocado Soup)

After savoring this soup in many of the great kitchens of Mexico, the author made a special, speedy adaptation for a health-food addict and staked its Mexican heritage with a touch of tequila.

2 ripe avocados (pared and pitted)
3 small white onions, chopped
½ cup heavy cream
¾ cup water
¼ cup white tequila
1 teaspoon soy sauce
1 teaspoon herb salt or seasoning salt
½ cup light cream
Salt to taste
Grated lime rind (for garnish)
Finely chopped almonds (for garnish)

Blend the avocados, onions, and cream to a smooth paste. Add remaining ingredients up to salt and blend to a smooth puree. Adjust the seasoning with salt and add more water if the consistency is too thick.

Chill the soup thoroughly and serve very cold. Garnish with a sprinkle of grated lime rind and very finely chopped almonds. (4 servings)

# Tequila Consomme with Tortilla Garnish

3 egg whites
6 cups strong stock made with 6 cups water and 6 teaspoons
    meat glaze or Bovril
½ cup dry red wine
¼ cup dry sherry
¼ cup tequila añejo
2 tablespoons tomato paste
2 bay leaves
Salt to taste
⅛ teaspoon cayenne pepper
1 tomato, unskinned and chopped
2 tortillas

Beat the egg whites until they are stiff. Put them in a pan and add the remaining ingredients, except the tortillas. Stir the mixture over moderate heat until it comes to a boil. Remove the pan from the heat and let it sit undisturbed for 15 minutes. Line a colander with a damp cloth and strain the consomme through it.

Cook the tortillas, roll them tightly, and cut them into thin strips. Put a few tortilla shreds in the bottom of each serving bowl and ladle the hot consomme over them. (4 to 6 servings)

# Shrimp Bisque

*Fish stock*

1-2 pounds fish bones and heads
5 cups water
1 carrot, sliced
1 onion, sliced
1 stalk celery, sliced
1 bay leaf
1 sprig parsley
4 peppercorns
¼ cup white tequila
½ cup dry white wine

*Bisque*

6 tablespoons vegetable oil
2 carrots, finely diced
2 turnips, finely diced
1 onion, finely chopped
8 green beans, finely diced
Salt
Freshly cracked white pepper
1½ pounds raw shrimps, in the shells
¼ cup tequila añejo
½ cup dry white wine
6 tablespoons rice flour
3 cups fish stock (above)
¾ cup butter
2 cups light cream
Cayenne pepper
Paprika

First, make the fish stock: Put the fish bones and heads in a pan with the water. Bring the water to a boil slowly and skim.

Add the other stock ingredients and boil down to 3 cups in quantity. Strain. Heat 1 tablespoon vegetable oil in a large heavy pan and add the diced carrots, turnips, onion, and green beans. Season with a little salt and freshly cracked white pepper. Cover the pan and cook very slowly until the vegetables are soft. Add the raw shrimps and saute for a few minutes. Heat the tequila in a little pan, ignite, and pour it over the shrimps and vegetables. Add the white wine and cook slowly for 8-10 minutes. Remove the shrimps and set them aside to cool.

Add the rest of the vegetable oil to the vegetables in the pan. Off the heat stir in the rice flour. Then add the fish stock. Stir the mixture over moderate heat until it comes to a boil. Reduce the heat and simmer gently for 10 minutes.

Set aside about a third of the shrimps. With the remaining two thirds, remove the tails and feet and coarsely chop the shrimps. Put the chopped shrimps with the shells, ¾ cup of butter, and a little of the stock mixture in the blender and blend to a smooth puree. Stir this shrimp butter into the rest of the stock and vegetable mixture, little by little, over very low heat. Then rub the mixture through a vegetable strainer.

Return the strained soup to the heavy pan and stir in the light cream. Add the cayenne pepper, paprika, and adjust the seasoning with salt. Shell and devein the reserved shrimps and cut them into very thin slices. Add them to the soup. (4 to 6 servings)

# Onion Soup

4 large Bermuda onions
3 tablespoons vegetable oil
6 tablespoons sweet butter
1 teaspoon finely chopped garlic
2 teaspoons potato flour
3 teaspoons meat glaze or Bovril
1 teaspoon Dijon mustard
4 cups water
½ cup dry white wine
½ cup tequila
Salt
Freshly cracked pepper
¾ cup freshly grated Parmesan cheese
6 slices French bread

Skin and cut the onions into thick slices. In a deep, heavy pan, heat the vegetable oil with 3 tablespoons butter. When it is bubbling, add the onions and brown them very slowly. When the onions are a deep golden brown, add, off the heat, the garlic, potato flour, and meat glaze. Stir until the mixture is blended. Then add the mustard, water, wine, and tequila, and season with salt and freshly cracked pepper. Stir the soup over moderate heat until it comes to a boil. Reduce the heat and simmer gently for 15 minutes. Sprinkle about half of the grated cheese over the top of the soup and simmer another 10 minutes. Toast the slices of French bread in the oven. Melt the remaining butter in a small pan.

To serve, ladle the soup into individual soup bowls. Set a piece of toasted French bread on top of each serving. Sprinkle the rest of the grated cheese and a few drops of butter over each piece of bread and set the individual bowls of soup under the broiler to brown lightly. (4 to 6 servings)

# Midwestern Chili con Carne

The state of Texas is usually credited with the origin of chili con carne—it is not a Mexican dish. But there is also a Midwestern version which is quite different from the Texan and very good. With the great popularity tequila enjoys in the Midwest, it was bound to find its way into the chili pot, too.

3 tablespoons butter
1 pound ground beef
½ cup tequila
1 teaspoon finely chopped garlic
2 cups chopped yellow onions
1 or 2 16-ounce cans red kidney beans (amount optional)
1 2-pound can Italian plum tomatoes
About 4 cups tomato juice
Salt
Freshly cracked black pepper
Chili powder, according to taste

Melt the butter in a large heavy pan (about 6-quart capacity) and heat it until it foams and is golden  brown. Add the ground beef and brown it thoroughly. Heat the tequila in a small pan, ignite, and pour it over the meat. Add the chopped garlic and 1 cup of the chopped onions to the meat and cook over moderate heat until the onions are translucent.

Add the kidney beans, plum tomatoes, tomato juice, and mix well. Bring the mixture to a boil over moderate heat. Season with salt, pepper, and chili powder. Reduce the heat and simmer gently for about 1 hour, with the pan uncovered. Stir occasionally so that the bottom does not scorch.

Serve in soup bowls with a separate bowl of the remaining cup of chopped onion for garnish. (6 to 8 servings)

## Salsa Barbacoa (Barbecue Sauce)

1 12-ounce jar guava jelly
¼ cup tequila
2 teaspoons garlic, finely chopped
A few drops Tabasco sauce
½ teaspoon meat glaze (or 1 teaspoon Bovril)
2 tablespoons tomato catsup
2 tablespoons tarragon vinegar
¼ cup vegetable oil
1 small white onion, finely chopped
1 tablespoon Worcestershire sauce
Salt and freshly ground black pepper, to taste

Combine all of the ingredients in a pan and simmer over low heat for 15 minutes. Brush over ribs, steak, or chicken. (1½ cups)

## Seafood Shashlik

*Rice pilaf*

4 tablespoons butter
½ teaspoon finely chopped garlic
1 yellow onion, finely chopped
1½ cups long grain rice
3 cups water
2 teaspoons salt
Freshly cracked white pepper

*Shashlik*

1 cooked lobster,
   or 2 cooked lobster tails
1 pound raw salmon

1 pound raw shrimps, shelled and deveined
1 pound sea scallops
½ cup tequila
3 green peppers, cored, seeded, and cut into eighths
2 Bermuda onions, skinned, quartered, and separated into pieces
¾ pound firm white mushrooms
3 medium-sized ripe tomatoes, cut in quarters, not skinned
1 pound thinly sliced bacon
1 teaspoon finely chopped garlic
½ cup vegetable oil
Salt
1 bunch fresh, crisp watercress

First, make the rice pilaf: Preheat the oven to 350° F. Melt the butter in a deep heavy pan. Add the garlic and onion and cook over moderate heat until the onion is soft but not brown. Mix in the rice. Add the water and bring it to a rolling boil. Season with salt and pepper, cover the pan with a firm-fitting lid, and cook in the preheated oven for 30 minutes.

While the rice is cooking, prepare the shashlik. Cut the lobster and salmon into large chunks. Sprinkle the lobster and salmon pieces, together with the shrimps and scallops, with ¼ cup tequila and allow to marinate for about 10 minutes. Arrange a mixture of the fish, seafood, and vegetables into 6 groups. Wrap each piece of fish and seafood in a half slice of bacon. In an alternating pattern, thread the fish, seafood, and vegetables alternately on the skewers and arrange them on a broiler or jelly-roll pan. Warm the chopped garlic with the vegetable oil and brush over the shashlik. Sprinkle with a little salt and broil for 15 minutes, turning once.

To serve, warm a long platter and on it arrange a bed of the rice pilaf. Lay the skewers on the bed of rice and garnish with the watercress. Heat the remaining ¼ cup tequila in a little pan, ignite, and pour it over the skewers. (6 servings)

# Shrimp Newburg

1 cup sliced onion, carrot, celery
1 cup dry white wine
3 cups water
6 peppercorns
1 teaspoon salt, plus extra for additional seasoning
1 bay leaf
1 ½ pounds raw shrimp (unshelled)
4 tablespoons butter
½ teaspoon paprika
⅓ cup tequila añejo
5 egg yolks, beaten
2 cups heavy cream
1 teaspoon dry mustard
1 tablespoon freshly grated Parmesan cheese
Cayenne pepper
8 toasted bread triangles

Combine the sliced onion, carrot, celery, wine, water, peppercorns, 1 teaspoon salt, and bay leaf in a pan and bring slowly to a boil. Add the shrimp and simmer very gently for 15 minutes. Let the shrimp cool in the liquid. Remove the shrimp from the liquid and shell and devein them.

Melt the butter in a saute pan, add the shrimps, and saute them over high heat until they have browned a little. Sprinkle them with paprika and the tequila añejo and cook over moderate heat until the tequila has almost disappeared.

Beat the egg yolks until they are lemony in color. Put them in the top of a double boiler with the cream, mustard, and cheese. Stir until the mixture thickens. Season with a little salt and cayenne pepper. Add the shrimps and stir them into the sauce. Transfer the shrimp and sauce to a hot serving dish and arrange the triangles of toasted bread around the sides. Serve at once. (4 servings)

# Camarones al Tequila
## (Shrimps in Tequila)

5 tablespoons butter
1 pound raw shrimps, shelled and deveined
½ cup tequila
4 tablespoons all-purpose flour
1 teaspoon salt
⅛ teaspoon cayenne pepper
1 cup light cream or milk
¼ cup dry white wine

Melt 1 tablespoon of the butter in a pan, add the shrimps, and saute them. Warm ¼ cup of the tequila in a little pan, add it to the shrimps, and set aflame.

In a separate pan, prepare a thick bechamel sauce as follows: Melt the remaining 4 tablespoons of butter. Remove pan from heat, add the flour, salt, and cayenne pepper. Stir in the light cream or milk, the remaining ¼ cup tequila, and the dry white wine. Return the pan to the heat and cook the bechamel until it comes to a boil and thickens — stirring constantly. Reduce the sauce to a simmer and add the prepared shrimps. Continue simmering the mixture just until the shrimps are warmed by the sauce, then serve. (4 servings)

*(By Rosa and Guillaume Martin, Estoril Restaurant, Mexico City)*

# Baked Fish with Tequila

4-6 medium-sized tomatoes, skinned and sliced thin
4-6 medium-sized yellow onions, skinned and sliced thin
1 whole pike, red snapper, or bass, cleaned and gutted (Select
    size according to servings desired)
Lemon juice (1 tablespoon plus approximately 2 extra
    teaspoons)
Salt
2 teaspoons fresh oregano, finely chopped, or ½ teaspoon
    powdered oregano
½ cup white tequila
2 cups dry white wine

Preheat oven to 350° F. Arrange half of the sliced tomatoes and onions on bottom of a roasting pan. Wash the fish in water mixed with 1 tablespoon lemon juice. Dry the fish on paper towels and rub it with lemon juice, then with salt and the oregano. Place the fish on top of the bed of tomatoes and onions in the roasting pan. Cover the fish with the remaining tomatoes and onions. Pour in the tequila and the white wine. Bake for 35 minutes.

To serve, carefully place the fish on a platter. Adjust the seasoning of the remaining tomato and onion mixture as desired with salt. Spoon this mixture along one side of the fish on the platter. (4-6 servings)

*(By Lionel Braun, Wine writer and importer, New York)*

# Tequileros' Beef

2 pounds top round of beef
1 cup tequila
1 teaspoon thyme
1 bay leaf
2 sprigs parsley
1 small onion, thinly sliced
1 small carrot, thinly sliced

12 black peppercorns
3 tablespoons butter
2 baby white onions, finely chopped
½ teaspoon finely chopped garlic
2 teaspoons meat glaze or Bovril
1 teaspoon tomato paste
3 tablespoons all-purpose flour
2 cups chicken stock
Salt
Freshly cracked black pepper
⅓ pound sliced bacon, cut into ¼-inch shreds
12 baby white onions, skinned
1 tablespoon chopped fresh parsley

Cut the beef into 1½-inch cubes. Marinate it for 24 hours in a bowl with the tequila, thyme, bay leaf, parsley, sliced onion and carrot, and peppercorns.

Remove the meat from the marinade (reserve the marinade) and dry it between paper towels. Heat the butter in a deep, heavy pan and brown the pieces of meat on all sides. Strain the marinade and heat the remaining liquid (the tequila) in a small pan, ignite, and pour it over the meat. Remove the meat from the pan, and add to the pan the chopped onion, garlic, meat glaze, tomato paste, and flour. Off the heat pour in the chicken stock. Return the pan to moderate heat and stir until the sauce thickens. Season it with salt and pepper. Return the meat to the pan, cover with a firm-fitting lid, and simmer over low heat for 2½ hours, or until the meat is quite tender.

In a separate pan, saute the bacon shreds until they are crisp and light brown. Drain on paper towels and reserve the bacon fat. Put the 12 baby white onions in a pan with ½ teaspoon salt, cover with water, and bring them to a boil. Drain the onions immediately. Toss the blanched onions in a little of the bacon fat over high heat until they are lightly browned.

When the meat is cooked, transfer it to a serving casserole. Add the bacon and onions. Spoon over the sauce and sprinkle with chopped parsley. (4–6 servings)

# Beef Birds

1 ½ pounds top round of beef, cut into thin slices
5 tablespoons butter
6 chicken livers
2 fresh mushrooms, sliced
Salt
Freshly cracked black pepper
3 ounces cooked ham, cut into fine shreds
¼ cup plus 2 tablespoons tequila
½ teaspoon tomato paste
1 teaspoon meat glaze or Bovril
2 teaspoons potato flour
1 ¼ cups chicken stock
1 tablespoon guava jelly
1 bay leaf

*Grilled tomatoes*

3 small ripe tomatoes, cut in half
Salt
Freshly cracked pepper
2 teaspoons granulated sugar
½ teaspoon finely chopped garlic
¼ cup freshly grated Parmesan cheese
3 tablespoons breadcrumbs
2 tablespoons melted butter
1 teaspoon chopped fresh chives

*Potato rosettes*

4 potatoes, peeled
Salt
2 tablespoons butter
1 egg
Pepper
1 tablespoon melted butter

Make the beef birds: Put the slices of beef between 2 sheets of wax paper and pound them with the side of a heavy meat cleaver until they are very thin. Heat 1 tablespoon butter in a deep, heavy pan and quickly brown the chicken livers. Remove them from the pan and add another tablespoon butter. Add the sliced mushrooms with a little salt and pepper. Cook them briskly for 2 minutes. Slice the chicken livers and mix them with the mushrooms and shredded ham. Season with a little salt and pepper. Put a tablespoon of this mixture on each slice of beef and spread to cover. Roll up each beef slice, sealing in the sides. Tie each roll in two places, with kitchen string. Heat another 2 tablespoons butter in the pan and brown the meat on all sides. Heat 2 tablespoons tequila in a small pan, ignite, and pour it over the meat. Remove the meat from the pan while you prepare the sauce.

Add to the pan and blend well the remaining tablespoon of butter, the tomato paste, meat glaze, and potato flour. Off the heat pour in the stock and the remaining ¼ cup tequila. Stir over moderate heat until the sauce comes to a boil. Stir in the guava jelly, add the bay leaf, and adjust the seasoning with salt and pepper. Set the beef rolls in the sauce and cook over low heat for 45 minutes, covered.

Carefully remove the strings from the beef birds when they are cooked, and arrange them on a warm, shallow serving dish or platter. Strain over the sauce and garnish with grilled tomatoes and potato rosettes.

To make the grilled tomatoes, sprinkle the top of each tomato half with salt, pepper, a little sugar, garlic, grated cheese, breadcrumbs, and a few drops of melted butter, and brown under the broiler. Sprinkle chopped chives over tops.

For the potato rosettes, boil the potatoes in salted water until very tender, then drain. Beat them in a mixer until smooth. Then beat in the 2 tablespoons butter and the egg, and season with salt and pepper. Put the potatoes in a pastry bag fitted with a #8 or #9 star tube and pipe rosettes onto a cookie sheet. Brush with a little melted butter and brown under the broiler. (4-6 servings)

# Hamburger Grill

This hamburger grill is to be served on skewers, but it may also be made into patties, as described at the end of the recipe. Suggested garnishes for either the skewered or patty serving are grilled tomato halves (*see* recipe, page 132) and shoestring potatoes.

1 ¾ pounds finely ground lean beef
¼ cup finely chopped onion
½ teaspoon Worcestershire sauce
Salt
Freshly cracked black pepper
6 tablespoons tequila
6 chicken livers, cut in halves
½ cup melted butter
6 strips of bacon, cut in half
12 mushroom caps
6 strips toasted bread
A few clusters fresh crisp watercress

For skewers: In the mixer combine the beef, chopped onion, and Worcestershire sauce, and beat thoroughly. Season with salt and pepper. Heat 2 tablespoons tequila in a small pan, ignite, and add it to the meat. Beat the mixture to incorporate the tequila. Form the meat into small balls the size of walnuts. Dip the chicken-liver halves in butter. Set the meatballs and livers on a broiler pan or jelly roll pan and lightly brown them under the broiler. Heat the remaining 4 tablespoons tequila in a small pan, ignite, and pour over the meats. Wrap each chicken liver in a half slice of bacon. Thread the meats and mushrooms on 6 metal skewers in the following sequence: meatball, mushroom, chicken liver; then repeat and end with a meatball. Set the skewers on the broiler pan and brush them with the remaining melted butter. Grill for a few minutes under a medium flame, turning frequently. Serve on strips of toast brushed with a little melted butter. Spoon over any juices from the broiler pan. Garnish with a sprig of watercress. Grilled tomato halves (*see* recipe, page 132) and shoestring potatoes make delicious accompaniments.

For patty serving: (The chicken livers may be eliminated.) Make the ground-beef mixture and form it into 6 large or 12 small patties, in either size at least a good 1-inch thick. Heat 3 tablespoons butter in a large saute pan, and when it is very hot, cook the patties on each side. Heat 4 tablespoons tequila in a small pan, ignite, and pour it over the patties. Serve the patties on strips of toast brushed with melted butter, garnished with the watercress and, if you like, grilled tomatoes and shoestring potatoes. Spoon the pan juices over the patties. (6 servings)

# Meatballs

*These meatballs, made in the size of a walnut,may be served as an entree with buttered noodles or rice. Or they may be prepared in the size of a marble to serve as an hors d'oeuvre.*

1 pound ground beef
2 ounces ground lamb (or veal)
2 lamb kidneys
¼ pound liver (calf's or chicken)
About 6 tablespoons butter
1 onion, finely chopped
1 teaspoon finely chopped garlic
2 slices white bread soaked in a little milk
2 eggs, beaten
6 tablespoons tequila
1 tablespoon chopped mixed fresh herbs
          (3 parts parsley, 1 part tarragon, 1 part chives)
1 teaspoon dry mustard
1 teaspoon freshly grated nutmeg
Salt
Freshly ground white pepper
3 tablespoons all-purpose flour
1 teaspoon tomato paste
1 teaspoon meat glaze or Bovril
1 cup chicken stock
1½ cups thick sour cream

Put the ground beef, ground lamb or veal, lamb kidneys, and the livers through the fine meat grinder twice. Transfer the ground meat to the mixer. Heat 1 tablespoon butter in a saute pan and cook the chopped onion for a minute or two. Add the onion to the meat with ½ teaspoon chopped garlic, the soaked bread, beaten eggs, 2 tablespoons tequila, mixed fresh herbs, dry mustard, nutmeg, salt, and pepper. Blend the mixture thoroughly and adjust the seasoning. Wet your hands and roll the mixture into balls. Make them the size of a walnut for use as an entree or the size of marbles for hors d'oeuvres.

Heat 3 or 4 tablespoons butter in a large saute pan and brown the meatballs lightly. (Take care that the butter is not too hot, causing the meat to brown too quickly and form a hard crust.) When all of the meatballs have been cooked, carefully return them to the saute pan. Heat 4 tablespoons tequila in a small pan, ignite, and pour it over the meatballs. Transfer the meatballs to a warm casserole.

Add another tablespoon butter to the saute pan with ½ teaspoon chopped garlic and cook for 1 minute. Stir in the flour, tomato paste, and meat glaze. Off the heat pour on the stock. Stir the sauce over moderate heat until it comes to a boil. Then, using a wire whisk, gradually stir in the sour cream, spoonful by spoonful. Season the sauce with salt and freshly ground white pepper. Return the meatballs to the pan and simmer very, very gently for 15-20 minutes, for walnut size, or 10-15 minutes for marble size—no longer, because you want to keep the meatballs light and delicate; if they are cooked too long they become soggy and heavy. Carefully spoon the meatballs and sauce into a warm casserole. (4 servings, as an entree)

# Tequila Burgers

1 pound ground round steak
1 tablespoon coarse salt
2 tablespoons butter
¼ cup white or gold tequila
4 sturdy buns or English muffins
4 slices Bermuda onion
Green or red chili-pepper sauce
Tomato, onion, olives, parsley for garnish (optional)

Shape the ground meat into 4 equal-sized patties. On one side press some of the coarse salt into each. Heat a saute pan very hot and melt the butter in it. When the butter is golden brown, put the meat patties in the pan, salted side down, and brown very quickly. Turn them over with a spatula and brown the other side. Pour the tequila into the saute pan. Carefully ignite the sauce in the pan and let the flame burn out. Then spoon the pan sauce over the patties several times.

Split the buns and briefly toast them under the broiler. To assemble each of the four burgers: Put a meat patty on the bottom half of each bun. Spoon a little of the tequila pan-sauce on top, then add a slice of the onion, then some of the chili-pepper sauce, then the top of the bun. Serve. Garnish the plate with slices of tomato and onion and olives and parsley, if desired. (4 servings)

*Author's note:* The father of this recipe reports that steak au poivre finished in this manner, with tequila, is a sensation.

(*By Lionel H. Braun, Wine importer and writer, New York*)

# Veal Scallop Saute

6 thin veal scallops (½ - ¾ pound)
2 tablespoons butter
¼ teaspoon salt
⅛ teaspoon pepper
2 tablespoons minced onion
1 clove garlic, minced
¼ lb. fresh mushrooms, sliced
¼ cup chicken broth
¼ cup tequila
Pinch of dried thyme leaves
1 tablespoon minced parsley

In large skillet, quickly saute veal in butter. Sprinkle veal with salt and pepper and remove to heated platter. Keep in a warm place.

In the pan drippings, soften the onion and garlic. Mix in mushrooms, chicken broth, tequila, and thyme. Simmer until reduced and slightly thickened. Serve veal with the mushroom sauce. Sprinkle parsley over all. (3-4 servings)

*(From Consumer Products Division, Heublein, Inc. for Jose Cuervo Tequila)*

## Peasant Shashlik with Wild Rice

*Marinade*

2 tablespoons olive oil
½ cup tequila
4 tablespoons tarragon vinegar
Black and white peppercorns
A little salt
1 or 2 bay leaves
½ cup thinly sliced onion, celery, and carrot, mixed

Combine all ingredients in a pan and warm the mixture over very low heat for 4 or 5 minutes. Remove from the heat and allow to cool.

(This marinade may be saved and stored in the refrigerator for future use with other meats.)

*Shashlik*

6 lamb kidneys
2 pounds shoulder of lamb, cut into 1½-inch chunks
1 small eggplant, peeled
Salt
6 chicken livers
6 thin slices bacon
½ pound firm white mushrooms, medium size
2 green bell peppers, cut in quarters and seeded
½ cup vegetable oil
1 teaspoon finely chopped garlic
3 tablespoons tequila

Cut the lamb kidneys in half and remove the cores. Mix the chunks of lamb shoulder and the kidneys with the marinade and allow to marinate from 4-24 hours.

Prepare the skewers: Cut the eggplant into 1½-inch cubes,

sprinkle them with salt, and allow to stand for 30 minutes. Dry the cubes between paper towels. Drain the meat from the marinade and store the marinade. Cut the chicken livers in half and wrap each in a half slice of bacon. Divide the meats, the eggplant, and the remaining vegetables into 6 groups and thread them on 6 metal skewers. Lay the skewers on a broiler pan or jelly-roll pan. Warm the vegetable oil and chopped garlic with a little salt for 2 or 3 minutes and brush this mixture over the skewers. Cook under the broiler for 10–15 minutes, turning once.

*Wild rice*

1 cup wild rice
Salt
2 tablespoons butter, melted
½ cup pine nuts, or ¼ cup sunflower seeds
½ cup white raisins
A few grains cayenne pepper

Boil the rice for 13½ minutes in an ample amount of salted water. Drain well. Line a large wire strainer or colander with a damp cloth and put the rice in it. Set the strainer with the rice over a pan with a little water in it. Cover the rice with a cloth and allow it to steam for about 15–20 minutes, until it is soft. Return the rice to the pan and add the butter, pine nuts or sunflower seeds, raisins, and cayenne pepper. Warm the mixture over very low heat for 5 minutes, stirring occasionally.

To serve: Arrange the wild rice on a large shallow serving dish that has been warmed. Lay the skewers over the rice. Heat 3 tablespoons tequila in a small pan, ignite, and pour it over the skewers. (6 servings)

# Breast of Chicken with Lime Sauce

4–6 boned chicken breasts
Enough all-purpose flour to coat chicken, plus 3 tablespoons
 flour
8 tablespoons butter
½ cup tequila
Finely grated rind of 2 large or 3 small limes
2 teaspoons finely chopped garlic
1 teaspoon tomato paste
1 teaspoon meat glaze
1 cup chicken stock
Salt
Freshly cracked white pepper
1 cup sour cream
1 cup heavy cream, whipped
Juice of 1 lime
2 teaspoons granulated sugar
1 teaspoon guava jelly
¼ cup grated Parmesan cheese

Dust the chicken breasts lightly with flour. Heat 5 tablespoons of the butter in a large saute pan. After it starts to foam, quickly brown both sides of the chicken breasts in it. Ignite with half of the tequila (¼ cup). Remove the chicken breasts from the pan and set aside.

Add the remaining 3 tablespoons of butter to the pan. Add the grated lime rind and chopped garlic and cook very slowly for 2–3 minutes. Remove from heat and stir in the tomato paste, meat glaze, the remaining 3 tablespoons of flour, chicken stock, and the remaining ¼ cup of tequila. Season with salt and freshly cracked white pepper. Return pan to medium heat and stir the sauce just until it comes to a boil. Reduce heat to simmer. Fold the sour cream into the whipped cream and stir this into the sauce, spoonful by spoonful. Add the lime juice, sugar, and guava jelly. Adjust the seasoning with salt and pepper to taste. Put the chicken breasts back in the pan, cover with the sauce, and cook over low heat 15-20 minutes, until they are tender.

To serve, arrange the chicken breasts in an au gratin or shallow serving dish. Spoon the sauce over them, sprinkle with Parmesan cheese, and brown under a hot broiler. Do not leave under the broiler too long or the sauce may separate. (4-6 servings)

# Pollo Almendrado
# (Chicken with Almonds)

1 whole chicken (3½-4 pounds)
Salt
4 tablespoons vegetable oil
½ cup white tequila
1 large onion, sliced
3 or 4 garlic cloves, chopped
3 chilies mulatto (black), veins removed and coarsely cut
3½ ounces raisins
6 ounces toasted, blanched almonds
1 large tomato, skinned and chopped
1 French dinner roll, toasted and crumbled
1 cup dry sherry
1 cup stock or water
½ cup vinegar
¾ cup green olives

Rub the chicken with salt and securely tie it with string. Heat the vegetable oil in a deep, heavy pan. When the oil is hot, brown the chicken in it on all sides. Pour in the tequila and ignite. Remove the chicken and set it aside for a moment.

Combine the sliced onion, garlic, chilies mulatto, and

raisins on a cutting board or in a chopping bowl and chop together. Put this mixture in the pan with the oil. Add to the pan the chopped almonds, tomato, and crumbled toasted French roll. Then add the sherry, stock or water, and vinegar. Stir the mixture and bring it to a boil. Return the chicken to the pan, cover with a firm lid, and cook slowly, either on top of the stove or in the oven, until the chicken is tender.

When the chicken is cooked, remove it from the pan and carve into serving pieces. Arrange the pieces on a serving platter and keep them warm.

In a blender, blend the pan sauce until smooth. Return the sauce to the pan, adjust the seasoning with salt, if necessary, and add the green olives. Warm the sauce a little and spoon over the chicken. (4-6 servings)

*(From Señora Gloria Sierra de Prieto, hostess extraordinaire, Mexico City)*

## Saucy Chicken Cutlets

3 chicken breasts, split, boned, and skinned
2 tablespoons butter
½ teaspoon salt
¼ teaspoon white pepper
2 tablespoons minced onion
1 clove garlic, minced
¼ cup tequila
¼ teaspoon dried tarragon leaves
1 cup heavy cream

In a large skillet, brown chicken in butter. Cover pan and cook chicken until tender (about 10-15 minutes), then sprinkle with salt and pepper. Remove to heated platter and keep warm. Soften the onion and garlic in pan drippings. Mix in tequila, tarragon, and cream. Simmer, uncovered, until sauce is reduced and slightly thickened. Serve chicken topped with sauce and garnished with chopped parsley. (4-6 servings)

*(From Consumer Products Division, Heublein, Inc. for Jose Cuervo Tequila)*

# Chicken (or Duck) Margarita

*Chicken*

1 orange
1 4-pound chicken (or duck), with liver
1 garlic clove, bruised
3 or 4 peppercorns
Salt
4 tablespoons melted butter
Small amount (about 1–2 tablespoons) bitter marmalade

*Basting mixture*

⅓ cup tequila
⅔ cup water

*Sauce*

2 tablespoons butter
2 tablespoons plus ¼ cup tequila
Rind of 2 oranges (finely shredded, lengthwise)
2 teaspoons finely chopped garlic
1 teaspoon tomato paste
1 teaspoon meat glaze
2 teaspoons potato flour
½ cup marsala wine
½ cup chicken stock or water
½ cup orange juice
½ cup bitter marmalade
Freshly cracked white pepper
2 teaspoons guava jelly
Skinned sections of 2 oranges

Preheat oven to 375° F. Make the basting mixture and set aside. Quarter the orange. Set the chicken liver aside and put the orange quarters inside the chicken, along with the garlic clove, peppercorns, and a little salt. Tie the chicken and put it on a rack in a roasting pan. Brush the chicken with the melted butter and pour a little of the basting mixture to cover the bottom of the pan. Place the chicken in the preheated oven and roast for 1 hour and 50 minutes, basting every 20 minutes with the tequila and water mixture. When the chicken has been in the oven for 40 minutes, turn it over on its breast. Leave it for 20 minutes, then turn it back on its back. Ten minutes before the chicken is finished roasting, spread the breast with a little of the bitter marmalade.

While the chicken is cooking, make the sauce: Melt 1 tablespoon of butter in a saute pan. When it is golden brown, brown the chicken liver, previously set aside, in it. Set the liver aflame with 2 tablespoons of tequila.

Remove the liver from the pan. Add to the pan the remaining 1 tablespoon of butter, shredded orange rind, and chopped garlic. Cook very slowly for 2 minutes without browning the orange rind and the garlic. Off the heat stir in the tomato paste, meat glaze, and potato flour. When it is smooth, mix in the marsala, chicken stock, the remaining ¼ cup tequila, orange juice, the bitter marmalade, and a little freshly cracked pepper. Stir the sauce over medium heat until it comes to a boil. Slice the chicken liver and add to sauce. Stir in guava jelly and simmer for about ½ hour. Add the orange sections.

When the chicken is ready, carve it into serving pieces and arrange on a platter. Spoon over the sauce. (4 servings)

## Poulet Mallorca

1 3½-pound chicken
10 tablespoons butter
¾ cup white tequila
Shredded rind of 2 oranges
2 teaspoons garlic, finely chopped
2 teaspoons tomato paste
2 teaspoons meat glaze
4 teaspoons potato flour
2 cups chicken stock

½ cup dry white wine
2 teaspoons guava jelly
½ pound mushrooms, thickly sliced
1 teaspoon lemon juice
2 green peppers, cut into large dice
Salt
Freshly cracked white pepper
3 large tomatoes, skinned, seeded, and cut in quarters
Skinned sections of 3 large navel oranges

Preheat the oven to 375° F. Tie the chicken with kitchen string. Melt 4 tablespoons of the butter in a deep, heavy pan until golden brown. Brown the chicken on all sides. Pour ¼ cup of tequila over the chicken and ignite. When the flame subsides, remove the chicken from the pan.

In the same pan, add 2 tablespoons of butter, the orange rind, and 1 teaspoon of the chopped garlic. Cook very slowly for 3 or 4 minutes without browning the garlic and the orange. Remove from heat and stir in the tomato paste, meat glaze, and potato flour. When the mixture is smooth, add the chicken stock, wine, the remaining ½ cup tequila, and the guava jelly. Stir the sauce over medium heat until it comes to a rolling boil. Carve the chicken into serving pieces and put them in the sauce in the pan, basting the chicken with the sauce. Put the chicken on the top shelf of the preheated oven and cook for 45-50 minutes, basting again once or twice.

While the chicken is cooking, prepare the following mixture: In another heavy pan or saute pan, heat the remaining 4 tablespoons of butter to foaming. Add the mushrooms, lemon juice, the remaining 1 teaspoon of garlic, and the diced green peppers. Season with salt and pepper. Cook briskly for about 3 minutes (the pepper should still be crunchy). Add the tomatoes and orange sections. Warm the mixture briefly; longer cooking will cause the tomatoes and orange sections to disintegrate.

Transfer the cooked chicken to a serving casserole. Spoon over sauce and vegetable-fruit mixture. (4 servings)

# "Chicken" Itza

Many people will remember the name Dione Lucas, once credited by Craig Claiborne in the *New York Times* as "the high priestess of high cooking in America." Dione Lucas was trained as a teacher by Henri Pellaprat, at l'Ecole du Cordon Bleu in the 1930s. Marion Gorman, coauthor of *The Tequila Book,* was the privileged heiress of all of Mrs. Lucas's files and library upon her death in 1972. One of the sentimental treasures was Dione's notebook of recipes from her student days. And there among the galantines without ado or explanation was this Mexican surprise avec tequila!

In Mexico *Chichen Itza* is a place. In Paris, or wherever Dione learned of this dish, it apparently became the name for a French culinary interpretation of chicken a la Mexico. (In the notebook, in Dione's handwriting, it is impossible to determine whether the recipe is named "Chic*h*en Itza" or "Chic*k*en Itza.") Isn't it nice to know that the French applauded Mexico—from whence came such important basics as tomatoes, potatoes, chocolate, vanilla, and turkey, without which classic French cuisine would be unrecognizable?

*Chicken*

3 whole chicken breasts, split and boned
½ cup white tequila
Salt
Pepper
5 tablespoons butter
2 chicken livers

*Stuffing*

2 tablespoons butter
½ teaspoon finely chopped garlic
¼ pound mushrooms, thinly sliced

1 teaspoon lemon juice
Salt
Freshly cracked white pepper
2 ounces boiled ham, finely shredded
1 tablespoon white tequila
Finely shredded rind of 2 oranges
¾ cup diced banana
1 tablespoon chopped fresh dill

*Sauce*

1 tablespoon butter
1 teaspoon meat glaze or Bovril
1 teaspoon tomato paste
3 teaspoons potato flour
1¼ cup chicken stock
½ cup white tequila
⅓ cup Madeira wine
½ cup dry white wine
1 teaspoon guava jelly
Freshly cracked white pepper

*Garnish*

2 tablespoons butter
3 bananas, split in half lengthwise
1 tablespoon chopped fresh dill

Cut a pocket in the side of each chicken breast. Open up the pockets and brush them with tequila. Set the remaining, approximately ½ cup, tequila aside for the time being. Season the chicken with salt and pepper. Close the pockets and let the breasts marinate while you prepare the stuffing.

Melt 2 tablespoons butter in a saute pan. Add the garlic, shredded orange rind, sliced mushrooms, lemon juice, and salt and pepper, and cook briskly for 3 minutes. Add the ham and 1 tablespoon tequila. Remove the mixture from the pan and chill it, then mix in the diced banana and chopped dill. Put a spoonful of this stuffing into the pocket of each chicken breast. Stuff them as full as possible, and reshape the breasts.

Heat 5 tablespoons butter in a large heavy frypan. When it is foaming, put in the stuffed chicken breasts, skin side down. Cover them with a flat lid or layer-cake tin, weighted to keep them flat. Brown on both sides. At the same time, add and brown the chicken livers. In a small pan, heat the ½ cup of tequila left from marinating the chicken, ignite it, and pour it over the chicken breasts and livers in the frypan. When the flame subsides, remove the chicken and livers from the pan and set aside.

Make the sauce: Add another tablespoon of butter to the pan. After it melts, remove the pan from the heat, stir in the meat glaze, tomato paste, and potato flour. When the mixture is smooth, add the chicken stock, ½ cup tequila, Madeira wine, white wine, guava jelly, and a little pepper. Stir over low heat until the sauce comes to a boil. Slice the cooked chicken livers very thin and add them to the sauce. Put the chicken breasts back in the pan, cover the pan with wax paper and the lid, and cook very gently over low heat 15–20 minutes, or until the chicken is tender.

While the chicken is cooking, prepare the garnish: Heat 2 tablespoons butter in a saute pan. Add the banana halves and cook briskly for 3 minutes only, turning once.

To serve, arrange the stuffed chicken breasts in an au gratin dish. Place a banana half on top of each breast. Coat the chicken with the sauce. Sprinkle a little chopped fresh dill on top of each banana half. (6 servings)

*(From Dione Lucas's notebook, kept during her student days at l'Ecole du Cordon Bleu, Paris)*

# Fruit Flamed in Tequila

4 tablespoons butter
⅔ cup brown sugar
4 peaches, peeled and sliced
¼ cup white or gold tequila

Melt the butter in a chafing dish or saute pan. After it starts foaming, add the brown sugar and stir until the sugar begins to dissolve. Add the prepared fruit. Spoon the pan sauce over the fruit until it has been warmed and the sauce is clear. In another small pan, warm the tequila and add it to the fruit. Ignite the sauce. Let the flame burn out and serve. (4 servings)

*Author's note:* This is very good served over a cooked grain, such as plain rice, whole wheat, oatmeal, or buckwheat. Also, other fruits, such as bananas, apples, oranges, pears, and mangoes, can be peeled and sliced and substituted for the peaches.

*(From Señora Beatriz Gonzales de Cue, Tequila de Viuda de Romero, Guadalajara, Mexico)*

# Tequila Lime Sublime

2 pints lime sherbet
½ cup tequila
4 limes

In a bowl, soften the sherbet with the tequila. Grate the rinds of 2 limes and add, with the pulp, to the sherbet mixture. Blend well. Spoon into dessert glasses and place in freezer for 2-4 hours, or until sherbet refreezes.

Slice the two remaining limes and slit each slice halfway through. When sherbet is frozen, hang a lime slice on the side of each glass and serve. (6-8 servings)

*(Anna Muffoletto / Cordon Bleu of New York, Ltd. for El Toro Tequila)*

# Mangoes with Tequila

16-ounce can of mangoes or peaches
4 tablespoons tequila
1 cinnamon stick (optional)

Drain mangoes or peaches and reserve the syrup. Put the syrup in a pan over heat, add the cinnamon stick if you wish, and reduce to one-half quantity. Add the mangoes to the reduced syrup and simmer until hot. Flame with the tequila. (4 servings)

*(By Baron Jay de Laval, Acapulco, Mexico)*

# Peaches of the Blushing Mayahuel

The name of this dish is typical of the poetic ingredient Gregory Thomas frequently adds to stimulate the taste buds in this homage to the goddess of tequila.

1 tablespoon butter
1 tablespoon granulated sugar
2 ripe, fresh peaches or nectarines, peeled and halved (or whole, deluxe canned ones)
1 tablespoon currant or raspberry jelly
1 8-ounce can mangoes, drained
¼ cup aged tequila
½ cup whipped cream
1 tablespoon slivered almonds.

Put a saute pan or chafing dish over medium heat. In the pan melt the butter and add sugar. When the sugar is dissolved, put the peach halves in the pan and spoon the syrup over them to glaze. Add the jelly and mangoes. Braise the fruit for a moment over low heat. Add the tequila to the pan and ignite.

To serve, put one or two peach halves and some mangoes on each dessert plate and spoon over some of the sauce. Top with a dollop of whipped cream and sprinkle with almond slivers. (2-4 servings)

*(By H. Gregory Thomas, extraordinary gourmet)*

# Peach Compote

4 large or 8 small firm ripe peaches
Rind of 1 orange, finely shredded
3 tablespoons butter
1 cup brown sugar
1 cup water
4 tablespoons tequila
Skinned sections of 1 or 2 oranges (for decoration)
A few blanched, split almonds (for decoration)

To neatly skin the peaches, pour boiling water over them, count to 17, remove and peel them. Cut them in halves and remove the pits.

In a deep, heavy pan combine the shredded orange rind, 1 tablespoon butter, and 1 tablespoon brown sugar. Stir over high heat until the mixture forms a thick syrup. Add ¾ cup brown sugar, the water, and 2 tablespoons tequila, and cook to a light syrup. Put the peaches in the syrup, reduce the heat, and simmer very gently for 10 minutes. Allow the peaches to cool in the syrup a little before serving.

To serve, transfer the peaches and syrup to a shallow silver or earthenware bowl. Decorate with neat orange sections and split almonds. Sprinkle with 2 tablespoons melted butter and the rest of the brown sugar and tequila. Set the dish under the broiler for a moment to brown lightly. Serve at once. (4 servings)

# Piña al Tequila
## (Pineapple with Tequila)

8 slices pineapple
3½ ounces white or brown sugar
4 ounces white tequila
1 quart vanilla ice cream

Coat the pineapple slices with the sugar and place them in a saute pan over heat. Allow them to cook until they become golden brown on both sides. Ignite the tequila and pour over the pineapple. Allow liquid in the pan to boil for three minutes. Serve over vanilla ice cream. (4 servings)

*(From Club de Industriales, Mexico D. F.)*

# Tequila Babas

16 baba molds, brushed with cool melted butter
1 rounded cup all-purpose flour
⅛ teaspoon salt
1 package dry yeast
¼ cup lukewarm water
3 large eggs, beaten
1 tablespoon sweet butter, creamed
1 tablespoon superfine sugar
2 tablespoons small black currants
3 tablespoons tequila añejo

*Syrup*

¾ cup water
1½ cups brown sugar
½ cup tequila añejo

Put the flour and salt in a warm mixing bowl. Dissolve the yeast in the lukewarm water. Add the beaten eggs and yeast and water mixture to the flour and beat lightly with your hand until the mixture is thoroughly blended. Cover the bowl with a plate and set it in a warm place to rise, for ¾ hour.

Preheat the oven to 375° F. Add the creamed butter, sugar, and currants to the dough, mixing them in with a rubber scraper. Half-fill the buttered baba molds with the dough and set them in a warm place until the dough rises to the tops of the molds. Bake the babas in the preheated oven for 15 to 20 minutes.

Make the syrup: Combine the water, sugar, and ½ cup tequila añejo in a pan and cook to 215° F. on the candy thermometer. Turn the babas out of the molds and put them in a large bowl. Pour the syrup over them and continue to repour the syrup over them until they have absorbed most of it.

To serve, arrange the babas on a warm serving plate. Heat the 3 tablespoons tequila añejo in a little pan, ignite, and pour it over the babas.

The babas may be put into a screw-top jar and stored in the refrigerator for several days. (16 babas)

# Souffle Cerro de Tequila
## (Hill of Tequila Souffle)

This is a delicious hot souffle, spirited with tequila and flavored with almond. In truth, tequila and almond are such a good marriage that in Mexico some of the tequila producers distribute a tequila liqueur, called crema de tequila, which is flavored with almond. Unfortunately crema de tequila is not available in the United States as of this writing. In Mexico this souffle can be made with crema de tequila instead of the straight tequila and almond flavoring ingredients as given in the recipe below.

*Souffle*

1-quart #6 souffle dish, lightly brushed with butter or vegetable oil
Wax paper
6 tablespoons almond meal (or finely ground almonds)
3 tablespoons butter
3 tablespoons all-purpose flour
¾ cup milk
2 tablespoons tequila
2 teaspoons almond extract
4 tablespoons granulated sugar
4 egg yolks, beaten
6 egg whites

*Sabayon sauce*

1 whole egg
1 egg yolk
5 teaspoons tequila
1 teaspoon almond extract
2 tablespoons granulated sugar

Preheat the oven to 375° F. Tear off a length of wax paper 1½ times the outer girth of the souffle dish, fold it in half lengthwise, and brush it with melted butter. Wrap the wax paper around the souffle dish and tie it with kitchen string. Dust the inside of the dish with 3 tablespoons of the almond meal. Set the souffle dish in a roasting pan and have a pan of hot water ready.

Melt 3 tablespoons butter in a saucepan. Off the heat stir in 3 tablespoons flour. Pour on the milk and stir over moderate heat until the sauce thickens. Then stir in the tequila and almond extract. Mix in the sugar and beaten egg yolks. Beat the egg whites to soft peaks and carefully and evenly fold the yolk mixture into the whites. Pour the mixture into the prepared souffle dish. Half-fill the roasting pan with hot water and set the souffle dish in the water bath in the preheated oven. Bake it for 30 minutes, or until it is just firm to the touch.

When the souffle is baked, carefully transfer the dish to a serving plate and remove the paper collar. Dust the top with the rest of the almond meal. Serve with a separate bowl of the following sabayon sauce:

Into a small bowl, put the egg, egg yolk, tequila, 1 teaspoon almond extract, and 2 tablespoons granulated sugar. Set the bowl in a small saute pan, half-filled with hot water, over low heat. Beat with a rotary beater until the sauce is foamy and stiff. Serve at once — this sauce will hold for 10-12 minutes. (4 servings) .

# Hot Lime Souffle

*Souffle*

1-quart #6 souffle dish, lightly brushed with butter or vegetable oil
Wax paper (buttered)
3 tablespoons granulated sugar plus additional for dusting
the dish
2 tablespoons sweet butter
3 tablespoons all-purpose flour
⅔ cup milk
Grated rind and juice of 2 large or 3–4 small limes
1 tablespoon tequila
4 egg yolks
6 egg whites
Salt
Confectioners' sugar

*Sabayon sauce*

3 egg yolks
3 tablespoons brown sugar
4 teaspoons tequila

Preheat the oven to 375° F. Tear off a length of wax paper 1 ½
times the outer girth of the souffle dish, fold it in half lengthwise, and brush it with melted butter. Wrap the wax paper
around the prepared souffle dish and tie it with kitchen string.
Dust the inside of the dish with granulated sugar. Set the
souffle dish in a roasting pan and have a pan of hot water
ready.
    Melt the butter in a saucepan and stir in the flour. Off the
heat add the milk. Stir over moderate heat until the mixture
thickens. Stir in the grated rind and juice of the limes, the
tequila, 3 tablespoons granulated sugar, and the 4 egg yolks.

Beat the egg whites with salt to form soft peaks and carefully and evenly fold the yolk mixture into the whites. Pour the souffle mixture into the prepared dish. Half-fill the roasting pan with hot water and set the souffle dish in the water bath in the preheated oven. Bake for 30 minutes, or until it is just firm to the touch.

To serve, set the baked souffle on a serving plate and carefully remove the paper collar. Dust the top quickly with confectioners' sugar. Serve with a separate bowl of the following sabayon sauce:

Put the egg yolks, brown sugar, and tequila into a small bowl. Set the bowl in a small saute pan half-filled with hot water. Set the pan over low heat and beat the sauce mixture with a rotary beater until the sauce is foamy and stiff. Serve at once — this sauce will hold for 10-12 minutes. (4 servings)

## Roast Stuffed Pork with Glazed Apples

1 piece loin of pork, 3½–4 pounds
1 tablespoon butter
2 small white onions, finely chopped
4 ounces ground veal
3 ounces sausage meat
1 raw egg white
½ teaspoon finely chopped garlic
2 tablespoons chopped fresh parsley
Salt
Freshly cracked black pepper
4 ounces sliced tongue, ½-inch thick
About ¾ cup tequila
2 teaspoons potato flour
1 teaspoon meat glaze or Bovril
1 teaspoon tomato paste
1½ cups chicken stock
2 teaspoons guava jelly
6–8 small red apples
¾ cup brown sugar
Rind of 1 orange, finely shredded
Juice and finely shredded rind of 1 lemon
½ cup water

Preheat the oven to 350° F. Bone the pork and spread it out
on a board. Heat 1 tablespoon butter in a small pan and saute
the onions until they are golden brown. Put the veal, sausage
meat, egg white, chopped garlic, and parsley in the mixer and
beat until well blended. Season with salt and pepper, and if
the mixture is too stiff, add a little cold water. Spread the
mixture on top of the pork. Cut the sliced tongue into finger-
size shapes and set them on top of the stuffing. Roll up the
pork and tie it in several places with kitchen string. Set it in a
roasting pan, sprinkle with a little salt and pepper, and pour

¼ cup tequila mixed with ¼ cup water around the meat. Insert a meat thermometer into the thickest part of the meat and roast to a temperature of 170° F., about 20-30 minutes per pound. Baste frequently with the juices from the bottom of the pan, and, if necessary, use more tequila and water mixed.

Now make the sauce. When the meat is cooked, remove it from the roasting pan and keep it warm. Remove all but 3 tablespoons of fat from the pan. Add ¼ cup tequila and stir until all the pan glaze is lifted. Off the heat add the potato flour, meat glaze, and tomato paste and stir to a smooth paste. Pour on the stock and stir over moderate heat until the sauce comes to a boil. Add the jelly and adjust the seasoning with salt and pepper. Reduce the heat and simmer gently for 10 minutes.

Glaze the apples: Peel the top halves of the apples and remove the cores. Put the sugar, orange peel, lemon juice and peel, water, and 2 tablespoons tequila in a deep, heavy pan and cook to a light thread stage, 225° F. on the candy thermometer. Add the apples, cover the pan, and cook slowly until the apples are tender but not broken.

To serve, cut as many slices of the pork as are needed for one serving. Arrange the slices overlapping down a warm oval platter. Place the uncut meat at one end. Pour a little of the sauce over the pork slices and serve the rest separately in a sauce boat. Garnish the platter with the glazed apples. Spoon a few drops of the syrup over each apple. Serve at once. (6-8 servings)

# Pork Chops with Pineapple

4 pork loin chops, 1 inch thick
1 garlic clove, bruised
A little all-purpose flour, for dusting
3 tablespoons butter
4 slices fresh pineapple, ¾ inch thick
⅓ cup tequila

*Sauce*

1 tablespoon butter
4 chicken livers
½ teaspoon finely chopped garlic
1 small green bell pepper, seeded and diced
½ teaspoon tomato paste
1 teaspoon meat glaze or Bovril
½ teaspoon potato flour
¾ cup chicken stock
1 tablespoon tequila
2 tablespoons guava or currant jelly
Salt
Freshly cracked white pepper

Rub the pork chops with the bruised garlic clove and dust them lightly with flour. Heat the butter in a large saute pan and brown the chops on each side. Reduce the heat and cook until they are done. Remove them from the pan. Quickly brown the pineapple slices over high heat. Return the pork chops to the pan. Heat the tequila in a small pan, ignite, and pour it over the pork chops and pineapple. Arrange the chops and pineapple slices alternately, overlapping, on a warm serving dish and spoon over the following sauce:

Add 1 tablespoon butter to the saute pan. When it is quite hot, quickly brown the chicken livers on both sides. Remove the livers and reduce the heat to moderate. Add the chopped garlic and diced green pepper and cook for 1 minute. Add the tomato paste, meat glaze, and potato flour, and blend the mixture. Off the heat pour on the stock. Stir the sauce over moderate heat until it is blended and thickens. Add the tequila and jelly, and season with salt and pepper. Reduce the heat and simmer gently for 10 minutes. Slice the chicken livers and add them to the sauce. (4 servings)

# Lomo de Puerco Tequila
## (Roast Loin of Pork with Tequila)

3 pounds boneless loin of pork
Salt
4 tablespoons lemon juice
½ cup tequila (white or gold)
1 cup cola

Preheat oven at 375° F. Rub the meat with salt and brush it all over with lemon juice. After the meat has marinated in its salt and lemon-juice coating for at least one hour, prick it all over with a fork, insert a meat thermometer, and place it in a roasting pan. Make a basting mixture of the tequila and cola and pour it over the meat.

Roast the pork in the preheated oven for 45–60 minutes, or until the thermometer indicates 170°. While the meat is roasting, baste it frequently with the tequila and cola mixture, mingling with the meat's roasting juices. Make additional basting mixture if needed.

When the meat is cooked, place on a serving platter and spoon the pan sauce over it. A mixed puree of potatoes and turnips makes a good, traditional accompaniment to the dish. (6–8 servings)

*(From Senora Sara Orendain, wife of Tequilero Roberto Orendain)*

# Chicken Tropicana

*Chicken*

2 small chickens, 2½–3 pounds, or 1 large, 5–6 pounds
1 clove garlic, bruised
A few sprigs of parsley
Salt
Freshly cracked white pepper
Butter (enough for the insides of the chickens, plus 3
    tablespoons)
½–¾ cup tequila
2 bananas

*Rice*

2 tablespoons vegetable oil
2 tablespoons chopped onion
½ teaspoon finely chopped garlic
1½ cups long grain rice
½ cup raisins (white or black)
3 cups chicken stock or water
2 tablespoons butter
1 cup sliced fresh mushrooms
1 teaspoon fresh lemon juice
½ cup finely diced, green bell pepper
½ cup sliced onions
2 tablespoons freshly grated Parmesan cheese
½ cup blanched, split, and browned almonds

*Sauce*

3 tablespoons vegetable oil
½ cup thinly sliced onion, carrot, and celery, mixed
3 tablespoons all-purpose flour
1 ripe tomato, sliced
1 teaspoon tomato paste

2 cups chicken stock
1 tablespoon guava or currant jelly
2 tablespoons tequila
1 tablespoon dry sherry
½ teaspoon meat glaze or Bovril
1 bay leaf
Salt
Freshly cracked white pepper
Bouquet of watercress or parsley (for garnish)

Preheat the oven to 375° F. Dry the chickens inside and out with paper towels. Put in each cavity a half clove of garlic, parsley, salt, pepper, and a lump of butter. Tie the chickens and rub them with a little more butter (on the breast and thighs). Set the chickens on a rack in a roasting pan. Mix ½ cup tequila with ½ cup water and pour it over the chickens. Insert a meat thermometer in one of the chickens and roast them in the preheated oven until they are tender (about 1 hour for 2 small chickens, or until the thermometer registers 185° F.). While the chickens are cooking, baste them occasionally with the pan juices, using more tequila and water mixture if necessary. When the chicken is cooked, remove the string. Using kitchen scissors, carefully cut out the entire breast section — the bone and meat. Then carefully remove the meat from each breast side, keeping it intact. Leave the oven at 375° F.

Make the rice mixture and use it to fill the opening in the chicken. Heat 2 tablespoons vegetable oil in a deep, heavy pan (one with a firm-fitting lid). Add the chopped onion and garlic and cook for 1 minute. Then add the rice and raisins and cook for 2 or 3 minutes, stirring constantly. Cover with the chicken stock and bring it to a boil. Cover the pan with the lid and set it in the hot oven or on top of the stove over low heat and cook for 25 minutes. Heat 2 tablespoons butter in a saute pan, add the sliced mushrooms and lemon juice and cook for 2 minutes. Add the finely chopped green peppers and sliced onions and cook for another 2 or 3 minutes. When the rice is cooked, fluff it with 2 forks. Add the mushroom, onion, and green pepper mixture, the grated cheese, and almonds. Round and smooth the top of the rice in the chicken cavities.

Cover the rice with the chicken and bananas: Slice the bananas diagonally. Heat 3 tablespoons butter in a saute pan. When it is very hot, quickly brown the banana slices. Halve each full chicken breast, then remove the skin from them. Cut the breast meat into neat slices, keeping them in order. Arrange alternate slices of chicken breast and banana on top of the rice, thereby reshaping the breasts of the chickens.

Warm the chickens in a low oven (250°) while you make the sauce. Heat 3 tablespoons vegetable oil in a saucepan. Add the sliced onion, carrot, and celery and cook for 3 or 4 minutes over low heat. Add the flour, sliced tomato, and tomato paste. Off the heat add the chicken stock. Stir the sauce over moderate heat until it comes to a boil. Then add the jelly, tequila, sherry, meat glaze, bay leaf, salt, and freshly cracked white pepper. Reduce the heat to a gentle simmer and cook until the sauce achieves a creamy consistency. Strain it.

To serve, arrange the prepared chickens on a warm serving platter and pour the sauce over them. Garnish with watercress or parsley. (4–8 servings)

# Breasts of Chicken Caroline

8 tablespoons butter
4-6 half breasts of chicken, boned and skinned
½ cup tequila
¼ cup sesame seeds, lightly browned and pulverized
½ teaspoon finely chopped garlic
4 ounces firm white mushrooms, sliced
Salt
Freshly cracked white pepper
1 can water chestnuts, cut in halves
1 teaspoon tomato paste
1 teaspoon meat glaze or Bovril
2 teaspoons potato flour
1½ cups chicken stock
1 teaspoon guava jelly
1 tablespoon chopped fresh chives or parsley

Heat 4 tablespoons butter in a deep, heavy pan. When it is foaming, put the chicken breasts in the pan and brown them on each side. Heat the tequila in a small pan, ignite, and pour it over the chicken breasts. Remove the chicken from the pan and set aside while you prepare the sauce.

Add the remaining 4 tablespoons of butter to the pan. Also add the pulverized sesame seeds and garlic and cook for 1 minute. Add the sliced mushrooms, season with a little salt and pepper, and cook for another minute. Add the water chestnuts. Then stir in the tomato paste, meat glaze, and potato flour. Off the heat pour on the chicken stock. Stir over moderate heat until the sauce comes to a boil. Add the jelly and adjust the seasoning with salt and pepper. Return the chicken breasts to the pan, cover, and cook over low heat until the chicken is tender. Do not allow them to overcook.

To serve, arrange the chicken breasts on a warm serving platter and spoon the sauce over. Sprinkle chopped fresh chives or parsley over the top.

*Author's note:* This dish may be accompanied with the rice pilaf recipe (*see* index).

# Curry of Chicken Wings

*Curry sauce*

1 tablespoon pure olive oil
4 tablespoons butter
2 cups chopped apple, carrot, celery, and onion (mixed)
3 tablespoons curry powder
3 tablespoons all-purpose flour
1 teaspoon tomato paste
½ teaspoon meat glaze
½ teaspoon finely chopped garlic
2 cups chicken stock
2 tablespoons tequila
1 tablespoon orange marmalade
2-inch piece cinnamon stick
Small piece ginger root
2 tablespoons shredded coconut
2 whole allspice
½ teaspoon freshly grated nutmeg
4 whole cloves
¼ teaspoon mace
1 teaspoon guava or currant jelly
1 small bay leaf
Seeds from a green pepper (see condiment listing)
Salt

*Chicken*

3 tablespoons butter
12 chicken wings, or 1 3½-pound chicken cut into serving
    pieces, or 6 half breasts of chicken
⅓ cup tequila

Rice pilaf, prepared according to the recipe given with the
Seafood Shashlik, page 126

*Condiments*

6 ounces sliced bacon, shredded, fried, and drained (reserve fat)
1 small avocado, peeled, and diced
Salt
1 small Bermuda onion, chopped
1 green pepper, diced
Shredded rind of 1 orange
2 hard-boiled eggs, peeled
Black and white raisins, mixed
Chutney
Shredded coconut
Salted peanuts

First, make the curry sauce. Heat the olive oil and butter in a heavy pan. When it is foaming, add the chopped apple, carrot, celery, and onion mixture and cook over low heat until the vegetables are soft. Stir in the curry powder and cook over low heat for 2 minutes. Blend in the flour, tomato paste, meat glaze, and garlic. Remove the pan from the heat and pour on the chicken stock. Stir over moderate heat until the seuce comes to a boil. Reduce the heat and add the tequila, orange marmalade, cinnamon stick, ginger root, shredded coconut, allspice, grated nutmeg, whole cloves, mace, guava jelly, bay leaf, and green pepper seeds. Adjust the seasoning with salt. Simmer the sauce for 45 minutes, stirring occasionally. Then rub it through a fine vegetable strainer.

While the curry sauce is simmering, cook the chicken. Melt the butter in a large saute pan and in it brown the pieces of chicken on both sides. Heat the tequila in a small pan, ignite, and pour it over the chicken. Cover the pan and cook over low heat until the chicken is tender.

Make the rice and keep it hot.

Before serving the curry, prepare the condiments in small, separate serving bowls or condiment dishes: Mix the bacon with the avocado and season with salt. Mix the reserved bacon fat with the chopped onion and add salt as desired. Combine the diced green pepper and shredded orange rind. Remove the hard-boiled egg yolks from the whites and chop and serve each separately. Put the remaining condiments in individual little bowls or dishes.

To serve, fluff the rice in a warm serving dish. Arrange the pieces of chicken on a warm, shallow dish and spoon over the sauce. Serve or pass the individual condiments. (4–6 servings)

# Appendix 1:

# Producers of Tequila

Avelino Ruiz, S.A., Arenal Jalisco, Mexico
Caballito Cerrero, S.A., Amatitan, Jalisco, Mexico
Destiladora de Occidente, S.A., Tequila, Jalisco, Mexico
Eucario Gonzalez, S.A., Tequila, Jalisco, Mexico
Elena Herrera Orendain VDA. de Camarena, Arandas, Jalisco, Mexico
Fabrica de Tequila la Union, S.A., Guadalajara, Jalisco, Mexico
Jaime Ruiz Llaguno, Atotonilco el Alto, Jalisco, Mexico
Jorge Ruiz Calderon, Arenal, Jalisco, Mexico
Jorge Salles Cuervo, S.A., Tequila, Jalisco, Mexico
Jose MA. Gonzalez Peña, Acatlan de Juarez, Jalisco, Mexico
La Madrileña, S.A., Atotonilco el Alto, Jalisco, Mexico
Licorera de Jalisco, S.A., Guadalajara, Jalisco, Mexico
Productos de Antano, S.A., Atotonilco el Alto, Jalisco, Mexico
Real Gusto, S.A., Guadalajara, Jalisco, Mexico
Rio de Plata, S.A., Guadalajara, Jalisco, Mexico
Salvador Ignacio Fonseca, Arenal, Jalisco, Mexico
Sanchez y Rosales, S.A., Arenal, Jalisco, Mexico
Sanchez y Sanchez, S.A., Zapopan, Jalisco, Mexico
Tequila Arroyo Bonito, S.A., Atotonilco el Alto, Jalisco, Mexico
Tequila Cazadores de Jalisco, S.A., Arandas, Jalisco, Mexico
Tequila Cuervo, S.A., Tequila, Jalisco, Mexico
Tequila el Viejito, S.A., Atotonilco el Alto, Jalisco, Mexico
Tequila Herradura, S.A., Amatitan, Jalisco, Mexico

Tequila Orendain, S.A. de C.V., Tequila, Jalisco, Mexico
Tequila Orendain en Mexico, S.A., Tequila, Jalisco, Mexico
Tequila Rosales, S.A., Tequila, Jalisco, Mexico
Tequila San Matias de Jalisco, S.A., San Jose de Gracia, Jalisco, Mexico
Tequila Sauza, S.A., Tequila, Jalisco, Mexico
Tequila Tapatio, S.A., Arandas, Jalisco, Mexico
Tequila Tepa de Jalisco, S.A., Tepatitlan, Jalisco, Mexico
Tequila Tres Magueyes, S.A., Atotonilco el Alto, Jalisco, Mexico
Tequila Virreyes, S.A., Tequila, Jalisco, Mexico
Tequila Viuda de Martinez, S.A., Tala, Jalisco, Mexico
Tequila Viuda de Romero, S.A., Tequila, Jalisco, Mexico
Tequilas Finos de Jalisco, S.A., Atotonilco el Alto, Jalisco, Mexico
Tequileña, S.A., Tequila, Jalisco, Mexico
Torres Perez Vargas, Hnos., Arandas, Jalisco, Mexico

# Appendix 2:

# The Marks of Tequila in the United States

Acapulco
Amigo
Arandas
Azteca
Beamero
Bravo
Bullfighter
Caballo Negro
Chiquita
Connoisseurs
Coronas
Corrida
Don Emilio
El Chico
El Charro
El Cid
El Grito
El Toro
Felicidad
Fiesta
Gavilan
Gold Label

Herradura
Jose Cortez
Jose Cuervo
Jose Gaspar
Juan Garcia
Juarez
Kelly y Gonzales
La Capa
La Prima
La Paz
Las Flores
Margarita Club
Mariachi
Matador
Montezuma
Newport
Old Mr. Boston
Old Mexico
Olé
Olmeca
Orendain
Pancho Villa

Papagayo
Pedro Domecq
Pepe Lopez
Puerto Vallarta
Rio Grande
Rosita
San Matias
Santiago
Sauza
Señor Chavez
Silver Pesos
Tavern F. Blanca
Terana
Torada
Tortilla
Valido Fresa
Valiente
Williams House
Yorktown
Zapata

# Index